Frozen Future

FROZEN FUTURE

The Arctic, the Antarctic and
the Survival of the Planet

DANIEL SNOWMAN

Random House

Toronto, New York, London, Sydney, Auckland

First published in 1993 by Random House of Canada Limited,
Toronto, and simultaneously in Great Britain by
Hodder & Stoughton Limited

Canadian Cataloguing in Publication Data

Snowman, Daniel

Frozen future

ISBN 0-394-22240-7

1. Polar Regions.   I. Title.

G.587.S66 1963   919.8   C93-093256-0

Photoset by E.P.L. BookSet, Norwood, London

Printed and bound in Great Britain

10   9   8   7   6   5   4   3   2   1

Contents

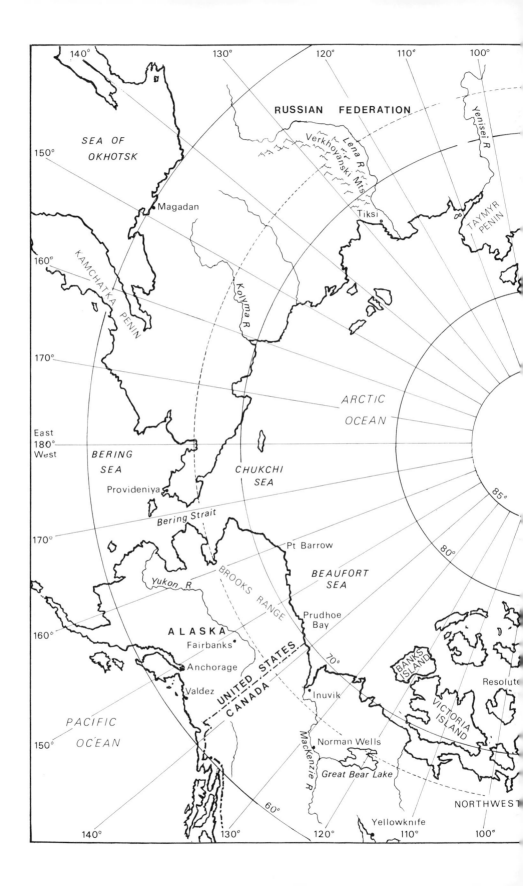

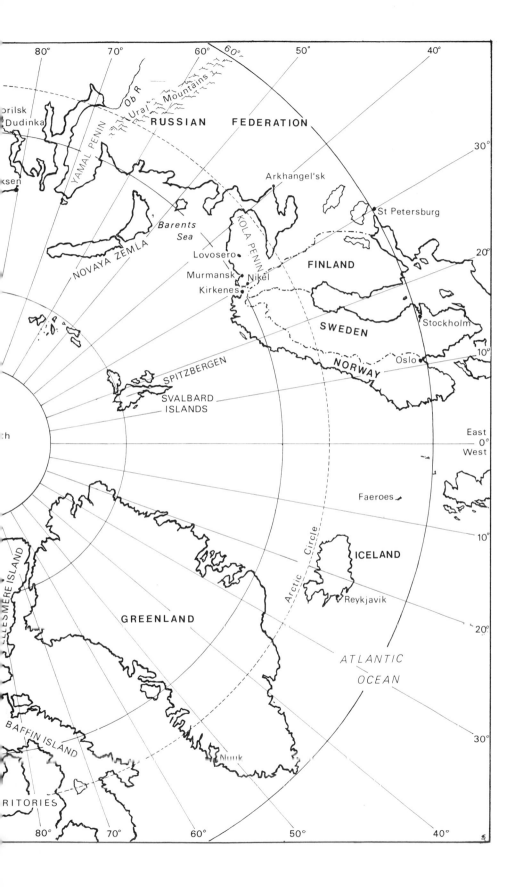

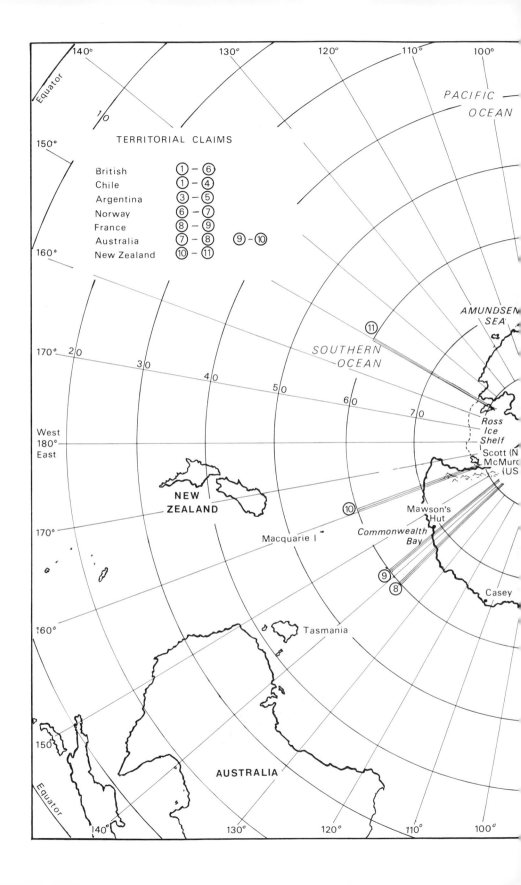

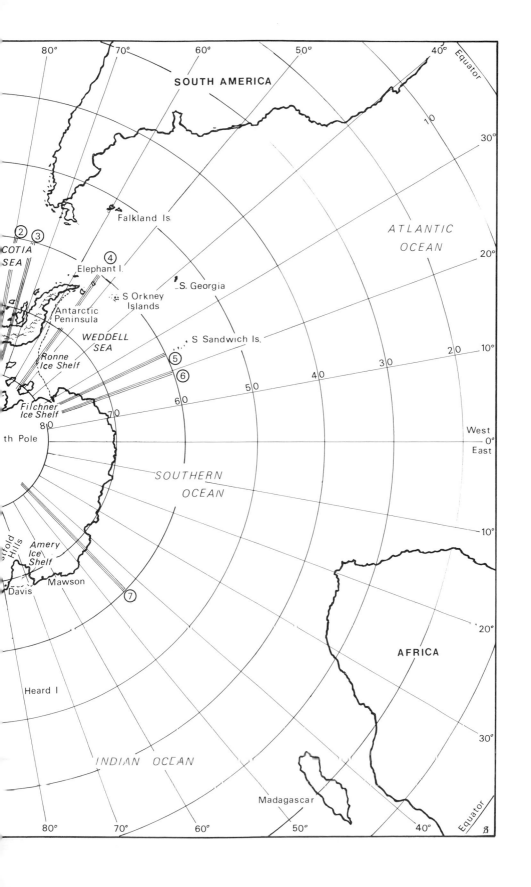

Photographic Credits

The author and publisher thank the following for the use of their photographs:
Birger Amundsen, pp 84, 168, 174; Australian Antarctic Division, pp 90 (left), 91; Mark Bendeich, pp 40, 90 (right); James Shevlin, p 142; Leslie Stephenson, p 98.

All other photographs are by Daniel Snowman.

Foreword

A thousand years ago, as the first millennium drew towards its close, prophets of doom proclaimed the imminent end of the world, and a paler version of this kind of *fin de siècle* fatalism has tended to recur at the end of each century since. As we approach the year 2000, there are many candidates for legitimate concern: nuclear holocaust, world population explosion and accompanying famine, an AIDS epidemic, genetic manipulation and abuse, global warming resulting from the greenhouse effect. These are large issues, united by a feature highly characteristic of our times: the fear that our scientific and technological temerity has gone too far and aroused the ire, and will perhaps produce the nemesis, of nature. It is science – global, macro-science – that excites and frightens people today.

None of these fears is trivial, but of them all the most awesome are those that concern not just the people on earth but the globe itself. After all, if we manage to avoid blowing ourselves up, keep world population within manageable limits, find a cure for AIDS and breed responsible geneticists, this would count for little if we bequeath our heirs an earth that is uninhabitably hot or cold, wet or dry. Thus, environmental issues are rapidly coming to assume higher priority and governments until recently oblivious of the dangers of chlorofluorocarbons or leaded petrol are now keen to appear 'Green'. My contention is that the governments and peoples should also learn to think 'White'. For it is in the vast but little-known polar regions that the key to the future of the planet probably lies.

The Arctic and Antarctic are two of the greatest deserts on earth, the least known and the most vital to our survival. They are in many ways, as well as literally, polar opposites. The High Arctic is a sea surrounded by land, Antarctica a

11

mountainous continent surrounded by ocean. The Arctic sustains an indigenous population of Eskimos (or Inuit) and others: nobody except a few scientists with extended supply lines can survive for long in Antarctica. Politically, the Arctic is largely controlled by the nations whose lands it contains; the Antarctic is neutral, demilitarised territory, subject to an international Treaty with to date some forty signatories. There are polar bears only in the North and penguins only in the South.

In a deeper sense, however, the poles meet. The Arctic and Antarctic act together as the earth's refrigerator, helping to drive the world's weather system and controlling nine-tenths of its stock of fresh water. Both contain clues, moreover, hidden beneath a thick layer of permafrost in the North and an almost impenetrable ice sheet in the South, about the early history of the planet and perhaps thereby of mankind. There are undreamed-of riches in the polar regions for the meteorologist and geologist, the biologist and palaeontologist; tempting opportunities, too, for the military strategist and mineral speculator, both of whom have been at work in recent decades in the North but whose activities have been restricted in the South by the workings of the Antarctic Treaty.

For centuries the poles have exerted a powerful fascination on the minds of the curious and the predatory and have often, Siren-like, lured the unwary to their deaths. Today the paths are better trodden, the stakes more clearly defined, the dangers better known – and the potential rewards greater than ever.

My own journeys around the top and bottom of the world have been by many forms of transport, among them dog team and skidoo (or snowmobile), ship, dinghy, plane, train and helicopter. I have met polar people – native northerners, and the scientists, engineers and others who come out from warmer climes. I have encountered something of the economics and working conditions of the Far North and Far South, come across examples of the ways in which mineral resources have been both used and abused around the Arctic and learned of the new environmental concerns in Antarctica, including the decision to ban mining. From economics and environmentalism the focus moves to polar science, particularly its contribution to our understanding of climate change and the large questions about the interrelationships between global warming and polar ice. Finally, circumpolar politics.

Both polar regions have provided the setting for competing sovereignty claims and national rivalries in the past, yet both seem at present to be in some ways models of international co-operation.

Throughout, whether we are considering the economics or the politics of the polar regions, the science or the indigenous peoples, one theme constantly recurs: the beauty and fragility of the polar environment – and its fundamental importance to the future of our planet and all it supports.

I have visited both East and West Antarctica and most of the countries around the Arctic rim. Grateful thanks are due to the British Antarctic Survey, the Australian Antarctic Division and the BBC for those opportunities. Also to Birger Amundsen with whom I travelled through Arctic Norway, Russia and around the magical island of Spitsbergen; to the many expert colleagues, friends and acquaintances quoted in the text; and to Peter Beck, Maureen Bundgaard, Louise Crossley, Bob Headland, Paul Laird, James Shevlin and David Wynn-Williams for reading portions of the manuscript and helping to weed out early errors and infelicities. Thanks, above all, to friends and family back home who tolerated with so much patience my recurrent physical and mental peregrinations to faraway places.

Finally, a few words about terminology. The native northerners of Alaska are for the most part happy to refer to themselves as Eskimos, while those of much of Arctic Canada and Greenland tend to consider this a pejorative term and prefer the word 'Inuit' (singular: 'Inuk'). Those in northern Quebec and Labrador are often 'Innu'. Native people of northern Scandinavia and the Russian Kola peninsula, widely known as Lapps, usually refer to themselves nowadays as 'Sami'. In the USA people commonly talk of temperatures in degrees Fahrenheit, elsewhere in Centigrade or Celsius. Most British and Americans still tend to measure distances in feet and miles, most Australians (and virtually all scientists) in metres and kilometres. Rather than try to iron out differences of this kind I have in general tended to adopt local usage.

CHAPTER ONE

Introduction

Think of the world as a giant Christmas pudding with a dollop of icing over the top and a far larger dollop spread across the bottom. The icing on a Christmas pudding is an optional luxury; that at the top and bottom of the world is essential to our survival. The Antarctic icecap contains ninety per cent of the world's ice and plays a major part in maintaining world temperatures and sea levels, while beneath the stormy Arctic seas between Greenland and northern Norway the surface waters plunge deep and initiate a system of global oceanic currents which include the Gulf Stream that warms Western Europe. If the polar regions were to warm significantly, rain-fall and sea levels could rise with catastrophic results, while a colder earth could bring year-round ice and permafrost to Oslo and Ottawa, Moscow and Montreal.

Until recent times most people who did not actually live there thought of the polar regions as remote places about which they knew, and needed to know, little or nothing. A few early European explorers had penetrated northern Canada and the Russian Arctic in search of furs, and some tried to navigate the Arctic Ocean in a series of fruitless searches for the North-east and Northwest Passages. Antarctica was bigger, further, colder; well into the eighteenth century it was still depicted on maps variously as a giant ocean, a continent, or, simply, 'Terra Incognita'. In the 1770s Captain James Cook boldly circumnavigated what we now know to be the Antarctic continent but did not actually see or touch it, much less try to explore it. In the nineteenth century, navigators stepped gingerly on to the Antarctic continent or pushed their way into the Arctic sea-ice. Some were whalers whose work led them naturally towards the ends of the earth; others were naval captains in pursuit of personal and national glory. The British, during the decades after the Napoleonic Wars, perhaps

14

seeking employment for their large and now idle officer class, sent one expedition after another across the Atlantic and off up the Canadian coast with instructions to find the Northwest Passage. Money and lives were often squandered in the attempt, though much of the north Canadian coastline and archipelago were successfully charted as a result.

By the beginning of the twentieth century, many thought the acme of ambition was to conquer the Poles: to reach them, that is, and be photographed there with a national flag. The attainment of the (North) Pole, said Robert Peary, represented "the last great geographical prize which the world has to offer to adventurous men". And he liked to claim, at least in public, that his principal motivation for trying to reach the Pole was that it "spells national prestige". By now, many nations were involved in polar research and exploration: imperial powers like Britain and France, countries with a direct practical interest like Russia and Norway – and the major newcomer on the international scene, the USA. Two Americans, Peary and Frederick Cook, squabbled over which (if either) had been the first man to reach the North Pole, while a Norwegian and an Englishman, Amundsen and Scott, each led teams to the South Pole a couple of years later.

Nowadays, with our vastly greater knowledge about the polar regions, we take for granted the answers to many of the mysteries that baffled Peary, Scott and their predecessors. Today's polar inhabitants and visitors can (unless they deliberately choose otherwise) live in some degree of comfort and safety, wearing clothes and eating food carefully adapted to harsh polar conditions and sleeping in warm and dry accommodation. In the sky above, satellites monitor cloud and sea-ice conditions and at the touch of a switch will radio down the results. The United States has a permanent scientific base (Amundsen–Scott) at the South Pole while, if you have the money, you can buy a tourist ticket to the Arctic that includes a flying visit to the North Pole. Many intrepid adventurers have continued to explore the polar regions by foot; an Englishman, Robert Swan, was the first, and so far the only, man to have walked to both Poles. But nowadays even the footsloggers do not have to go without proper clothing and a two-way radio set; you can be resupplied and, if necessary, evacuated by aircraft.

In many ways the polar regions have become demystified.

Superb television films have been shot in the ice kingdoms of north and south and scientists live in comfortable conditions for months and even years at a time in regions once thought by most Europeans to be virtually uninhabitable. The indigenous peoples of Alaska and northern Canada have acquired not only TV and video sets but also an active political consciousness and there are signs that *glasnost* has brought something of the same to their Siberian counterparts. On several occasions I have spoken by telephone from ships deep in Antarctic waters to the BBC in London – and then picked up those same conversations, edited into World Service radio programmes, on the ship later the same day.

Modern technology has brought a degree of familiarity to the remote and the inaccessible that would have confounded Scott and Amundsen. We know about the dangers of global warming, and worry about deforestation in Brazil and ozone depletion in the stratosphere. And where science and technology lead, the language of popular discourse follows. We learn new words, phrases and acronyms (the ozone hole, the greenhouse effect, CFCs, PCBs) almost as though by incorporating the words and phrases into our vocabulary we are somehow rendering the phenomena themselves more manageable.

New answers, however, suggest new questions. We may know the shape of the north Canadian coastline and the benefits of wearing several thin layers of clothing rather than woolly long johns; we may be able to see iceberg patterns on a radar screen before we reach them. But what of the deeper questions about our world? Many scientists believe that locked away within the icy elements of the Arctic and Antarctic lie clues to some of the most fundamental enigmas about the universe we inhabit. If you want to investigate the age of the planet, for example, or its long-term climatological trends or the basic movements of land and sea – you would be well advised to start at or near the ends of the earth.

There can be no doubt about the vital importance of polar science in an age that has had to learn about ozone depletion and the greenhouse effect. Here, spectacularly, are two global trends, researched by polar physicists, which have possible implications for the long-term fate of humanity that can scarcely be exaggerated. But even at the more superficial level of personal observation, any visitor to the polar regions is quickly made aware of changes coming over our planet. I remember sailing south through the Scotia Sea in the far South Atlantic on the British Antarctic Survey ship the RRS *Bransfield* in March 1988, the late Antarctic summer. I was travelling with Bernard Jackson for a series of BBC radio documentaries we were making together. Already, just a couple of days out of Stanley in the Falklands, as we sailed towards the South Orkneys, we began to meet literally hundreds of small icebergs – 'bergy bits' or (even smaller) 'growlers' – where twenty or thirty years before, according to some of the old hands on board, the seas would have been relatively clear of ice. Is the Southern Ocean getting *colder* perhaps? Not a bit of it, they replied. The seas were colder a century ago when any icebergs the ships encountered at these latitudes would probably have been of a more substantial size. No. What these dangerous chunks of ice pointed to, they said, is that the really large bergs further south that calve off the great Antarctic ice shelves appear to break up earlier at more southerly latitudes than in the past because the waters in which they float tend if anything to be warmer than in previous years.

You might even see this happening. One morning as we moved carefully through icy waters, we sailed a few hundred metres from one of those vast floating islands of ice that have intrigued travellers since the time of Cook and earlier: a great marble sculpture gleaming in the bright southern sky. As I watched, the entire island began to submerge at a perilous angle into the dark waters and, to the accompaniment of an unearthly wrenching sound, shed its lowest part and righted itself again in the water. Where one iceberg had towered a minute before there were now two, mother and calf. All birth is a mystery. But the reasons why that iceberg split into two at that particular time and place lead directly into fundamental questions about the changing geophysical processes of the planet.

Closer to the poles other questions press themselves forward. The Antarctic continent is covered by a permanent sheet of ice, in places three to four kilometres thick. Could global warming cause this (and the Greenland ice sheet) to melt, thus raising world sea levels and flooding low-lying cities like London or Tokyo? The quick answer is that Antarctic temperature variations do permit some surface melting, but that this tends to be quickly absorbed into an atmosphere that is permanently dry and windy (and often sunny). So there is little danger, yet at any rate, of large amounts of water being emptied into the oceans. As a matter of fact, the initial impact of melting the surface of the Antarctic icecap could, if anything, be for local sea levels to *fall* as the mass of ice the sea had to support was reduced. Little of this is in any case yet observable. What *may* be happening is that atmospheric warming could cause increased evaporation rates over both polar regions and produce more precipitation over the warmer edges of the ice sheet – and this, allied to oceanic warming of the underside of the edges of the great ice shelves, could contribute to more ice breaking off as icebergs. At the fringes of the ice sheets stretched across Greenland and Antarctica, therefore, there may be an acceleration of the pace at which glacier ice breaks off to become icebergs – the beginnings of the process that I saw at a later (i.e. more northerly) stage in 1988 in the Scotia Sea.

Much of this is speculation. But there is no doubt about the importance of finding out what is happening to the 'icing' at the top and bottom of our global Christmas pudding. Is it really receding, or melting, and, if so, why? Are the polar regions warming up, along with the rest of the world, as a result of the greenhouse effect – indeed, are the Arctic and Antarctic Oceans warming faster than, say, Europe or the Americas because of the absorptive properties of water? Or more slowly because ice reflects solar radiation back away from the earth? Perhaps we are merely coming out of the Little Ice Age that caused the Thames to freeze over in the seventeenth and eighteenth centuries.

If the polar regions *are* getting warmer, might there not be beneficial by-products? For example, the Russians talk of permitting international cargo shipping through the Arctic Ocean from Murmansk to the Bering Straits. If the ice of the Northeast Passage is becoming more navigable, this could prove a far quicker route from northern Europe to Japan than going through Suez. And the people of sub-Arctic Canada, for example, will presumably stand to gain if a more benign climate enables arable farming to be practised in their region. This, in conjunction with increased economic development, could lead to a shift in Canada's population pattern away from the notorious clustering close to the US border – and as pollution of the Great Lakes increases and water levels fall, Canada's hitherto frozen north might become an increasingly valuable source of fresh water.

Over ninety per cent of the world's stock of fresh water is in solid form, most of it on the Antarctic and Greenland ice sheets. This slowly feeds the great polar glaciers and finally calves off to form the giant icebergs whose remains we have already encountered in warmer seas. But how does this process of ice-calving interact with the great oceanic currents that wash and warm our shores? These currents are in part initiated in the two great regions where freezing polar seas encounter warmer waters from more temperate climes: in the north Atlantic off the coast of Greenland and northern Scandinavia, and down south in the Antarctic Convergence — especially near the Weddell Sea. In these rough and remote seas, the denser cold surface water plunges to the depths, taking huge quantities of dissolved gases and minerals to the ocean bed. This process helps to cycle gases like carbon dioxide that are noxious to animal and human life, while at the same time supporting the micro-organisms in the water column and on the ocean bed that form the basis of the global food chain. It also drives the world's oceanic currents, including the Gulf Stream that warms Western Europe. As our emissions of carbon dioxide continue to increase, however, some scientists believe that the absorptive capacity of the oceans may no longer be able to cope. Now, carbon dioxide is a greenhouse gas; if more of it remains unabsorbed by the oceans and the biota they contain, while the air above the polar seas gets correspondingly warmer, the temperature contrast with temperate waters will diminish. If this happens, it could adversely affect the great plunge in the northern and southern seas that drives the world's ocean currents. In this way, excessive carbon dioxide emissions could threaten the eventual vitality of the Gulf Stream. By making the earth's atmosphere warmer, therefore, we may alter the pattern of oceanic currents — and eventually make the oceans colder.

Thus, great global trends with which our scientists are grappling do not all point in the direction of a world getting warmer. In some ways, indeed, the scientific indicators point towards colder seas and a cooler planet: a larger dollop of ice at top and bottom. Glaciologists believe we are between two ice ages. Does this prognosis contradict those who speak with confidence about the greenhouse effect? Not necessarily since the timescales for the two tendencies are very different: if both sets of predictions prove accurate, we – or our successors – could fry (or drown) before we freeze. We may also starve – not just because the world will contain too many people for the available food to go round, but because in addition the basic oceanic food chain may be at risk.

Here, too, polar scientists have been among the first to reach for the alarm bells. In the Southern Ocean, for example, some have suggested that there is a superabundance of the very basis of the marine food web, the micro-organisms that form phytoplankton. This is what feeds the shrimp-like krill whose swarms sustain the larger marine animals like penguins, seals and whales and ultimately the great sub-Antarctic fishing banks. For two centuries and more, man has severely disrupted the natural balance in the polar seas: first, by hunting the seals and then the whales almost to extinction, and more recently by indiscriminate overfishing. The Japanese and Russians, having hoovered the seas of herring and cod, have also turned to krill as a possibly commercial proposition. The great polar oceans could soon be as empty of fish as the once teeming North Sea and Mediterranean.

But nature has also been at work, sometimes almost overcompensating for these human depredations. Where there are too few whales there will be too much krill; where there is too much krill – particularly near rocky outcrops that may be warmer and greener than they once were – seals will swarm and overbreed. Around the coast of the little island of Signy in the South Orkneys, for example, there were only a few hundred fur seals as recently as the 1970s. When I visited in 1988 they were everywhere. Much the same is true as far north as Bird Island off South Georgia and Heard Island in the sub-Antarctic sector of the Indian Ocean, where seals rear up, snorting, barking, baring their fangs and exhaling their smelly breath at you. Their numbers and movements have eroded much of the tussock grass so that, as you thread your way across the lumpy terrain, fur seals are at first sight almost indistinguishable from the muddy hummocks on which they wallow. On Signy Island there are now so many fur seals – in excess of 16,500 – that they are in danger of swamping an already overcrowded habitat. As one little sub-Antarctic island becomes populated to the point of discomfort, seals

20

will swim greater and greater distances to find space elsewhere: an ironic sequel to the massive slaughter in the nineteenth century.

There are somewhat similar tales to tell in the Arctic about the disruptive interactions between man and animal. Some have a provisionally happy ending: the Canadian musk ox, for example, almost extinct a century ago, is now a thriving and protected species. But elsewhere things take on a more ominous tone. In northern Scandinavia, the sub-Arctic Sami (or Lappish) peoples have for centuries built up a rich culture centred on one animal: the reindeer. This provided not only the staple food of the Sami but their principal material for clothing and means of transport. It was also a major cultural symbol, giving rise to a large vernacular vocabulary untranslatable into any non-Sami language. But a combination of circumstances – political discrimination, the spread of a cash economy, and the harmful effects of radiation from Chernobyl – has seriously weakened the reindeer culture of the Sami people. Some believe that reindeer herding as a way of life may not survive as the bewildered Sami gradually succumb to the money, jobs and housing many have received as compensation.

The Arctic rim has substantial indigenous populations with interests often at variance with those of the explorers, scientists, missionaries, conquerors and variegated predators and entrepreneurs who have all stamped their mark upon the region. The native peoples of the Arctic are of course just as interested as their visitors in resources and trade routes and in whether the planet is getting colder or warmer. But many also face a conflict between a traditional way of life based on hunting and trapping and the more settled, modern life-style recently brought in from the south. Whether among the Sami of Lapland or among the native peoples of Greenland, North America or Siberia, the story is the same. "They put us in wooden houses, give us television sets and tell us to send our children to school every day," says an elderly Innu living in northern Labrador sadly, "and now the youngsters don't want to go out and hunt."

In some ways the problems faced by the Canadian Inuit, the Sami of northern Scandinavia or the Siberian Nentsy or Eveny are similar to those faced in any Third World country by rapid modernisation. In Lapland or Labrador, just as in Botswana or

Brazil, youngsters become excited by rock music and fast food (and drink), while their parents sense a valued and traditional way of life slipping from their grasp. But the indigenous peoples of the north have additional problems: physical isolation, an inhospitable climate and a fragile culture easily vulnerable to the allure of literacy, Christianity or modern medicine. Above all, they lack the political strength that comes from physical contiguity; no African colony would have achieved independence if its people had been scattered throughout the continent and beyond. These problems were highlighted when, for example, the Americans began oil-prospecting off Alaska's Prudhoe Bay or NATO ran low-flying missions out of Goose Bay in Labrador – two undertakings that seemed sensible enough to hard-headed governments and their official representatives but which brought major changes to the fragile life-style of the local communities.

However, northern peoples everywhere are acquiring increased political consciousness and self-confidence. Greenlanders obtained a large degree of autonomy from the Danes in 1979. In the 1980s the Canadian government began to negotiate agreements with native groups offering rights over vast tracts of land in its northern territories to the indigenous communities. The political and economic implications for colonised and native peoples are obviously considerable, and in Canada itself, a country troubled by recurrent constitutional conflict between centre and peripheries, clearly momentous. Will the Inuit land transfers prove to be the first step towards the eventual establishment of a new province (or nation)? Across the Arctic Ocean, the Nentsy of northern Siberia, angered beyond endurance by the ravages of gas drilling, are demanding proper political representation to a degree that would have been a capital offence in the days of the gulag.

Politically and economically the Arctic is largely controlled by the 'rim' nations whose lands it contains. Disputes have tended to be local. The Canadians and the Americans have bickered about navigation rights in (and beneath) the waterways of the Canadian archipelago, the Norwegians and the Russians over the exact location of their boundary in the fisheries of the Barents Sea. For forty years after World War II much of the Arctic region was an armed camp as the Russians and the Americans squared off against each other across the top of the world. Today, the end of the Cold War has begun to open up a region formerly shrouded in secrecy so that Russians, Americans, Canadians and Scandinavians – and the native northerners from around the entire Arctic rim – are beginning to share resources in a way that would have been unthinkable a few years before. There is no overall Arctic Treaty comparable to that governing the Antarctic. But the nations and peoples of the north are learning to co-operate amicably almost as though there were one.

Global *glasnost* has been taking some intriguing turns. In 1989 the Russians sent delegates for the first time to the Arctic Games in Yellowknife (Canada), and in March 1990 hosted an international Inuit congress. There is now a standing Inuit Circumpolar Conference with representatives from every Arctic-rim nation, while serious proposals have been put forward to declare Siberia's Chukotskiy Peninsula and Alaska's Seward Peninsula (which face each other across the Bering Straits) an International Park with shared administration. As for the economics of the region, the Arctic has historically been of interest for two main reasons. The first is the resources it contains: biological ones (beaver pelts, seal oil, whale blubber); minerals (gold, zinc, uranium); and hydrocarbons (coal, gas, oil). The second attraction has been to people seeking trade routes. Three of the world's nine longest rivers flow through Russia northwards into the Arctic. Like the MacKenzie River in North America, these have long been important conduits of people and goods and have led their more intrepid navigators into wondering about the nature of the Arctic Ocean into which they spill. For centuries the quest for a navigable Northeast and Northwest Passage to the Orient bewitched the imagination of entrepreneurs from many northern lands. Today the dreams of Frobisher and Willoughby, of Hudson, Franklin and Nansen, may at last become reality.

A world away lies the Antarctic, altogether a more awesome and forbidding prospect than its northern counterpart. Antarctica, a land mass nearly twice the size of Australia, surrounded by ocean, is far larger than the Arctic region, and considerably colder. Here there are no people, except temporary visitors. At the Amundsen–Scott base at the South Pole, the Americans routinely register winter temperatures of −50°C, while the Russians at their Vostok base once registered a record −89.2°C. Nobody can live in Antarctica unless supported from outside, and on the Antarctic continent itself only very specialised and sparse flora or fauna can survive.

Yet the Antarctic has come to attract even greater international interest than the Arctic. Partly this is because it is larger, grander, more inhospitable and even more beautiful than the Arctic. But there are practical as well as poetic reasons for the world's fascination with Antarctica – as a glance at the science that goes on down there makes abundantly clear.

The most famous recent outcome of Antarctic science is the identification by upper atmosphere physicists of the hole in the ozone layer, a phenomenon whose practical implications can scarcely be exaggerated. But it is not only the physicists and chemists whose work has captured the imagination. Antarctic geologists, for example, tell us that Antarctica was once the core of a vast supercontinent (Gondwana) that included all the southern hemisphere lands that eventually drifted off northwards. If you look at a globe of the world with the South Pole in the middle it is not hard to construct a mental jigsaw bringing together the jagged points of Latin America, southern Africa, India, the Malayan peninsula and Australia and linking them up with Antarctica. But behind the revelations about continental drift are messages full of practical promise to governments and companies shrewd enough to make the right inferences. The Chileans, for example, keen to replenish diminishing stocks of Andean tin, silver and other metals, have noted with interest that the Antarctic Peninsula and the Andes have a common origin. Might both not therefore contain similarly valuable mineral deposits?

A few years ago, palaeontologists uncovered marsupial fossils in Antarctica. This extraordinary find suggested not only a supercontinent that once linked Antarctica with Australia but also an Antarctic climate warm enough to support mammalian life. Seventy years earlier, Shackleton found fossils of tropical tree ferns in Antarctic coal deposits. Today, palaeobotanists working in Antarctica regularly collect fossils of the long-extinct *Glossopteris* plant, for example, that date back to Permian times some 250 million years ago, and similar fossils have been found in various other locations in the southern hemisphere, helping to confirm the Gondwana hypothesis. *Glossopteris* would have grown in warm, swampy forestland. Scientists have even found pieces of wood in Antarctica – not

24

fossilised wood from the Permian but actual wood a mere three million or so years old – twigs from a low, ground-hugging tree of the *Nothofagus* family that evidently flourished high up in the Transantarctic Mountains at 85°S. Was the Antarctic therefore once further north than now? Or is the world getting colder? Glaciologists digging for cores deep into the Antarctic ice sheet are able to read global temperature patterns back over thousands of years – not sufficient to tell us much about the climate of Gondwana or even at the time of those twigs from the Transantarctic Mountains, but enough to confirm that, at least according to previous patterns, we are probably heading slowly towards another ice age.

In the late 1950s, the nations with an active interest in Antarctica, including the USA and USSR, came together in the wake of the International Geophysical Year to create the Antarctic Treaty. They agreed to demilitarise the entire region below 60°S, freeze claims of national sovereignty, and make the results of their scientific work available to co-signatories. The Antarctic Treaty, planned to run indefinitely from 1961 but open to review thirty years later, was to prove an outstanding example of international co-operation. During the Falklands War of 1982, while their compatriots were killing each other, British and Argentine scientists continued to co-operate over Antarctica.

National political interests have not disappeared South of Sixty, however. Some observers have suggested that the Falklands War itself was fought in part at least to guarantee continued British access to a region of Antarctica over which Argentina might wish to assert future hegemony. Fanciful? Not when you reflect that a number of Argentine babies – the first Antarctic 'natives' – just happened to be born in the Argentine base at Esperanza on the Antarctic Peninsula directly south of the Falklands.

Nor was Argentina the only nation to go in for mildly provocative activities in Antarctica. Both the British and the French, for example, began to build airstrips in their respective Antarctic sectors during the late 1980s, despite complaints from Green organisations who wondered loudly whether these constructions were strictly necessary to the conduct of bona fide science. American aircraft arriving at Amundsen–Scott would routinely taxi 360° round the South Pole base, which some thought a symbolic assertion of American rights of access to every sector of the continent. And all this crypto-political posturing was observed by countries like Malaysia who asked with increasing vehemence why Antarctica should be governed by an exclusive Treaty and not by the United Nations.

The polar regions are among the last great wildernesses on an over-cluttered planet, natural laboratories for the study of some of the fundamental questions about the past, present and future of life on earth. Every day we read how world weather patterns show signs of altering, sea levels of rising and air of becoming irreversibly polluted. We are bombarded with sometimes contradictory data about global warming, ozone depletion, Arctic haze and the near annihilation of certain oceanic food stocks, and hear of indigenous peoples everywhere finding their traditional cultures menaced by the seductions of modernity. In a world under threat, the polar regions are becoming increasingly valued as fragile resources whose careful study and conservation may prove in every sense vital to our survival.

CHAPTER TWO

Getting There

The sheer scale of Arctic Canada almost defies imagination. Or, rather, the size relative to the number of people living there. Once in a while you might come across some sign of human habitation: a winter ice road perhaps; in summer time, a straight trail over the land itself might indicate earlier seismic work by an oil company. But for the most part there are no buildings, no paved roads, no divisions of the land into separate holdings. Just the vast unfolding of the land itself, much of it covered in winter time by a blanket of snow and ice. From the air, particularly from the jets by which many busy administrators from the Yukon and Northwest Territories commute around their huge domains, the land surface can seem largely undifferentiated, particularly in the dark winter; one expanse of snow and ice largely resembles another from 30,000 feet.

But come down from above the clouds, take a single-engine Cessna 185 or a Twin Otter, perhaps, or a helicopter at a couple of hundred metres and travel, ideally during the spring when the sun begins to emerge from its long hibernation and makes its first tentative efforts to free the land from its thrall of ice, and a world of differences is revealed in all its richness. In lower latitudes, particularly in the west, you might find yourself looking out over woodland stretching as far as the eye can see; a carpet of black spruce, larch, birch and willow. Not the dense, richly green forests of the temperate and equatorial regions to be sure. The woodlands of sub-Arctic Canada are more sparse, the vegetation drier and more brittle, the foliage clearly struggling for survival in a harsh climate, their roots tough but shallow in a thin topsoil above intermittent rock and permafrost. The trees themselves, stunted grey-green conifers giving the land the appearance of an unplucked chicken, often stand at a rakish angle to the ground, not so much because they are windswept as because their roots, needing to embed themselves securely in frozen bedrock, have had to scramble sideways in their attempt to establish viable foundations.

'Down but not out' was a phrase that crossed my mind as I drove along the Dempster Highway, the one major road in the north American continent to cross the Arctic Circle, with on either side as far as the eye could see rocky scrubland supporting (if that is the right word) scrawny spruce and branchless birch. By now you have left the boreal forest of the sub-Arctic, and the trembling aspen and balsam poplar give way to the thickets and heathers of the tundra, while the brave willows and dwarf birches that grow up here cling closely to their roots, often by now bending almost drunkenly horizontal in their desperate efforts to retain a roothold.

As you move still further north, these stunted forestlands grow even more sparse. At first, the wooded landscape might simply be interrupted by a series of lakes, still frozen perhaps, winking back at the welcoming sunlight. Or the ancient pre-Cambrian granite surface of the earth's crust may push itself aggressively out towards you, brushing any form of forestland out of its way as a giant brushes away flies. A few trees may be able to survive unswatted on the giant's chin. But, in general, the high ground of the North Canadian Shield sustains little woodland of any consequence. Here, mosses and lichens abound, clinging to the outcrops of rock and, in the low sunlight, trying out their spring colours.

Out west the treeline reaches a lot further north than in the Eastern Arctic and really polar conditions do not take hold until close to the Beaufort coast. On the slopes of northern Alaska, above some of the world's richest oil reserves, animals graze on tundra shrub that flowers throughout a brief but often quite warm summer. The Arctic Circle itself, that artificial line on the map above which there is twenty-four-hour sunlight in mid-summer and twenty-four-hour darkness in mid-winter, can, in the western part of Canada and the State of Alaska, experience quite benign temperatures even in early spring and late autumn.

But travel north across the bleaker, more frozen eastern part of Canada, across into the Keewatin region, perhaps, or up the east coast of the giant Hudson Bay, and you rapidly meet the Arctic head on. The lakeland that is northern Canada gradually gives up any pretence at being a solid land mass as the whole vast topography moves from lake-spattered land to an

Springtime on the still semi-frozen MacKenzie delta.

island-filled ocean. The legs and arms of this giant lakeland link up and, as you travel still further north, it seems only a question of time before water will predominate and create islands of land.

By now, the lakes are multiplying like amoebae, the visible manifestations of a continental drainage system that reaches its most dramatic form in the great MacKenzie River of the west and the giant Hudson Bay in the east. The amoebae multiply – an uncountable number of frozen lakes and ponds each with its own plethora of limbs, covering a surface that at times seems to consist of more water than land: islands of land set in a silver sea of gleaming ice rather than a lake-filled land surface. Indeed, this is what the topography of Canada becomes once you clear the northern coast and head towards the great archipelago of the High Arctic.

Think of the Arctic and what images emerge in the mind's eye? Vast white vistas of snow and ice with the occasional seal or walrus perhaps. Or a smiling Eskimo standing by his igloo, faithful huskies in attendance. The dog team is one of the great clichés of polar iconography, as essential to most armchair images of the Far North, and to some extent of Antarctic science and exploration also, as the beefeater or busbied guard

Shopping by skidoo at Resolute Bay for sealmeat to feed the dogs.

is to the tourist-poster image of London. And almost equally archaic. In many places around the Arctic rim, the 'iron dog' – the snowmobile or caterpillar-tracked skidoo – has become the most common form of transportation, while in the Far South, strict compliance with the Antarctic Treaty has meant that dog teams, by definition non-indigenous to the region, have been or are intended to be removed.

Yet the romantic image of the polar sled drawn by huskies is by no means obsolete. In Greenland, for example, dogs still prevail in most townships and settlements and even in Arctic Canada many people continue to argue the merits of dogs over any mechanical form of transportation.

"Dogs don't break. Skidoos break." The laconic comment of one Inuit hunter as he took me out over the ice one frozen night. Another pointed out that a dog team spread out ahead of you can act as an early warning system when you are travelling over thin ice or crevasses and indeed can jump over crevasses or help pull you out if necessary.

"Dogs can survive indefinitely on sealmeat," a third told me. "Where are you going to find gasoline for a skidoo out on the tundra?"

Huskies are also good to have around when you are in polar bear country. "A dog will bite the bear on the rear end, keep

30

the bear busy and distract it," a Canadian Inuk elder told me, and spoke with affection of a pair of dogs who had once saved his life in this way.

Another powerful argument for the maintenance of dogs is undoubtedly the bond of camaraderie that builds up between man and animal.

"I know every one of these dogs, their names and personalities, and they all know me." I was with Brent Boddy, a tall, strapping Canadian who lives in Iqaluit and who raised all his dogs from puppyhood. We were sitting on Brent's sled and ahead of us, hitched in fan formation and pulling us across the frozen surface of Frobisher Bay, was a handsome team of nine huskies, all positively yelping with excitement as they trotted across the ice.

"They seem happy," I observed to Brent as we slid across the frozen surface of the Bay.

"Running with the sled," he laughed, "is one of their three greatest thrills in life" – leaving me to guess what the other two might be.

A few years before, Brent and his dogs had accompanied the American expeditioner Will Steger to the North Pole, the first group to achieve the Pole taking everything with them – i.e. unsupported by air drops on the way – and the first to include a woman in the team. Brent was originally a westerner, from Edmonton, Alberta, attracted to the Arctic by tales he heard from Inuit friends about its scale and beauty. Today, there is nowhere else he would prefer to be. "From my house I can go one hundred miles in almost any direction," he said, sweeping his arms imperiously from his position atop the sled, "and travel in some of the most spectacular scenery anywhere on earth. You can see over huge areas in this clear, more or less unpolluted air," he added, "and yet see hardly any sign of humanity."

We were sledding under a bright summer sun which infused the Arctic icescape through which we were gliding with a wealth of subtle shades of pink, blue and orange, an infinitely delicate palette of pastel beauty.

"Hey, hey!" barked Brent, as one dog near the middle of the fan ran into his neighbour's path. His voice had an edge of venom, and the offending animal was quick to return to its own patch. "When you run a dog team," Brent said, turning to me, "there's a lot of acting involved. You've got to convey to

31

the dogs not only what you want them to do but also that you're serious about it."

I sat in the back of the sled, a shallow wooden bathtub bobbing its way over the rough tidal ice of Frobisher Bay, and wondered how this experience compared with Brent's journey to the Pole. We were in temperatures of about −15°C which, with the wind chill, reached perhaps −25°C. I was wearing several layers of clothing but was still grateful for the caribou parka Brent threw over me. "On the journey to the Pole," he said, "temperatures were regularly in the minus fifties − and that's not including the wind chill!"

I was carrying a plastic bag containing camera and recording equipment. At the Pole, said Brent, the plastic bag would have solidified and shattered and the recording machine and camera mechanisms would probably have iced up. And even if they could still have functioned it would have been too cold for me to take off my gloves for more than a few seconds to operate them properly.

But some things are absolutely essential, even at −50°C. So I asked Brent the question that astronauts are always getting asked. How did you get *those* functions fulfilled?

"Basically, you have to plan ahead and work up a bunch of steam, so that when you decide to go − you've got just a few seconds to use your hands and you must be ready. Everything comes down to timing. At those kind of temperatures it's critical that you're always completely in tune with your body and that takes total concentration."

"When you say 'work up steam' − you mean that literally?"

"Oh yes, I mean, run, walk, help the dogs with your sled for a while − and these sleds were weighted down with 1,000 pounds each. Anything to build up heat ready for the few moments when you stop and do whatever you've got to do."

Sweat, however, is at best a mixed blessing at extremely low temperatures. It can render you temporarily warm, but often at the cost of making your body and thereby your clothes damp. And damp clothes at −50°C soon become icy clothes, a constant danger during polar journeys. "Every time you work," said Brent, "you build up moisture inside your clothes; and when you go into a warm tent and start cooking there'll be condensation that will saturate the outside of your clothes." Many of the polar explorers of the past recount occasions when they went to bed in a sleeping-bag that graduated during the night from warm to damp to frozen.

This kind of problem is less acute nowadays than in the days of Scott and Peary. When Will Steger and his team went to the Pole in 1986 they used sleeping-bags made of a special material that, sponge-like, sucked moisture out of their polar suits and helped the sleeper to emerge drier by morning. And the polar suits themselves were a lot more sophisticated than those available to their predecessors. Today's explorer will wear a relatively lightweight series of carefully insulated layers, possibly topped by animal skin or fur, where earlier generations tended to opt for thickness of covering. For your polar clothing must not only keep you warm. It must also allow you maximum flexibility of movement in order to keep perspiration at a minimum. "Getting damp is almost a greater hazard than getting cold," says Brent who has experienced both.

The change in the polar wardrobe is largely the result of new technology — new fibres and man-made materials, developments in our understanding of human physiology. But it is partly, too, the result of a change of attitude. Many early explorers to the polar regions, particularly to the more obviously accessible Arctic, would set out to conquer the Northwest Passage or the North Pole and pit the might of civilization against the hostile forces of the Far North. Expeditions would often be led by people with a military background and the values and rhetoric they would try to imbue in their men would be those of battle.

Like would-be conquerors everywhere, they were not especially concerned about the native peoples over whose territory they travelled. Some Arctic explorers were kind enough to local natives, some killed them, some sentimentalised them as noble savages. But very few until modern times had the sense to learn from them. When Sir John Franklin led his last, vast expedition to the Canadian High Arctic in the 1840s, he and his senior colleagues came dressed in their English finery, still expecting to live according to the style (and off the silver cutlery) of the British upper classes. It would have been distasteful for them to have had to share the diet, clothing or living conditions of the native Inuit, a climb down the ladder of civilization. Much less would they have bothered to learn the language. Going native would have been a sign of softness.

Later in the century, explorers like the American Charles

Francis Hall realised that they might have something to learn from the native people they encountered. The Inuit, after all, could evidently survive in a cold climate more successfully than most white visitors. They did not suffer from scurvy or frostbite. Maybe this was not a question of inherent racial characteristics such as skin pigment and the like, but had something to do with the kind of clothing they wore and diet they ate.

Thus, gradually, people like the Canadian Vilhjalmur Stefansson and the Danish-Greenlandic Knud Rasmussen lived with native communities when in the Far North, hunting and trapping with the Eskimo, eating caribou and seal, dressing in animal skins, living in sod huts and snow igloos. There were severe hazards to this kind of life, and social and sexual arrangements, for example, repulsive to most people from the south. But you learned to keep warm, and dry, and to eat an indigenous diet that was overwhelmingly better adapted to conditions in an extremely cold climate than the tinned and salted southern delicacies brought north in the ships of Franklin and others.

This is not the whole story. Whites have also been responsible for importing many other aspects of their essentially European culture to the high latitudes. You can now pray in a Protestant or Catholic church in the Arctic, eat lamb cutlets and oranges, and watch Hollywood movies or even live sports events on TV. And southern whites have imported other delicacies from the south, too, like coronary heart disease, cancer, dental decay and alcohol. Some of the social repercussions of increasing white familiarity with the peoples of the Far North make desolate reading. But at least few Europeans nowadays go to the high latitudes intending to do battle with nature, or to conquer; for they know now that nature will always win.

"Up here," Brent Boddy proclaimed, looking into the far distance as he spoke, "Mother Nature calls the shots. Everyone here lives with the flow, bends with it and adapts to it. You have to. If you don't you're lost."

Wisdom in the Arctic means learning from the people – and also from the wildlife of the region. All have developed ways of adapting to the harsh polar climate. Take the Canadian musk ox, for example, a scowling baby bison in appearance with a long shaggy coat and a formidable pair of centrally linked horns. Numbers of Canadian musk ox have fallen drastically during occasional periods of acute food shortage or exceptionally cold weather. But scientists point to their second layer of hair, a tight, insulating underwool called 'kiviut', which gives them powerful protection against the Arctic winter. Today in the Canadian Far North, out on Banks Island, people are learning to weave their own clothes out of musk ox kiviut and make themselves superthermal underwear directly derived from the example of the local fauna.

Brent Boddy loves the northern wildlife by which he is surrounded, and relishes going on long, exotic trips with his dogs. Indeed, he has turned what began as a hobby into a small business outfitting and accompanying visitors to the Arctic. One trip took him the whole length of Canada's Baffin Island – greater than the entire distance of Britain from south to north – through a number of tiny, isolated native communities and some of the most awesomely beautiful scenery in the world. "The only way to do a journey like that is with dogs."

He spat another vicious command at the dogs and cracked his whip alongside the fan. The huskies trotted on, their energy undiminished.

"These dogs couldn't win a race if their lives depended on it. They are Canadian Eskimo huskies and they aren't bred for speed but for strength and stamina: hunting, hauling heavy loads, taking nomadic peoples across huge distances. So they're very sturdy, very tough, adept at hunting. These dogs are doing maybe eight kilometres an hour – but they'll keep that up for ten hours at a time. That's eighty kilometres without stopping. They're like a boat – slow, but so long as you have patience, you can be sure you'll get there."

Their strength and tenacity are impressive, though the harmony of a good dog team can easily be disrupted by poor handling. The team and handler must both know which dog is boss. A good boss dog, like the leader of an orchestra, will help keep the rank and file in order and ease the occasional introduction of a new member into the team. He will keep his privileged position for perhaps seven or eight years – though only if he can retain his authority over the other dogs. This he will periodically assert by nipping a straggler on the ear, barking at a dog who has strayed from his path or making sure he gets fed first. If he loses his authority and the dogs overthrow him for another boss, his humiliation is total and he goes, as it were, to the back of the second fiddles.

If one of a husky's three great thrills in life is to go out running with the sled, one of the other two is to have a good feed when he is finished for the day. The prospect of being allowed to attack a banquet of seal or walrus meat produces a cacophony of expectant wailing and barking as the dogs, safely back on the chain, strain against their traces in ecstatic anticipation. A hungry husky will demolish in short order not just the meat itself but also the fat, the hide, and the calcium-filled bones with single-minded and muscular relish.

If you are fortunate enough to visit somewhere exotic and really distant the best way to go is slowly. In the era of instant electronic communications, jet travel and tight deadlines this is rarely feasible; who has the time, money and flexibility to undertake a Grand Tour nowadays in the leisurely style of the eighteenth century? Much of the inhabited Arctic is now reachable by plane, and even the vast icy remoteness of Antarctica has a handful of airstrips, including one used by the Americans at the South Pole. Several of the Treaty nations can now fly people and supplies to the fringes of the southern continent, though the economic and environmental costs of building and maintaining a safe and secure air link to a remote Antarctic station are beyond the wildest imaginings of all but the richest or most determined of governments.

One nation that is clearly determined to be a major Antarctic player is Australia. The area of Antarctic territory to which she lays claim is larger than that of any other claimant state: a slice of pie fully forty-two per cent of the whole. She also maintains several bases on Antarctica stretching over a region more than 3,000 miles across. For years the Australian Antarctic Division has debated the pros and cons of building a permanent air link. As elsewhere in Antarctica, winter landings on ice are feasible and can be used for local reconnaissance and emergency flying. But, for a combination of economic and environmental reasons, no permanent airstrip has been built. All Australia's Antarctic bases are therefore resupplied by ship, and every southern summer sees a busy schedule of sailings from Hobart across the southern waters of the Pacific and Indian Oceans to Australia's widely scattered Antarctic outposts. These are epic voyages, especially those that visit the westernmost stations of Mawson and Heard Island – locations far to the west of Australia itself, closer to Cape

Town than to Hobart and lying beneath Pakistan on the map.

Day after day you plough your lonely furrow through southern seas virtually devoid of other shipping. In most of the world's oceans you can have the security of knowing that somebody, somewhere, will be poised not too far away to help you out if you run into trouble. Another ship or two will show up on the radar. Birds will swoop in your wake suggesting land somewhere in the vicinity. But as you steer south and west from Australia thousands of nautical miles into the great Southern Ocean that girdles the lower latitudes of the planet, and make for the great white continent of Antarctica, you are truly alone as almost nowhere else on earth, and many an Antarctic voyager, tossing in his bunk with the corkscrew movements of the ship, must have wondered with Jonah whether God in His infinite wisdom really intended mankind to try and navigate these terrible waters. *Homo sapiens*, indeed, according to one of the safety videos you are required to watch by the Australian Antarctic Division before leaving Hobart, is essentially a tropical animal who can only survive in temperate regions, let alone polar ones, courtesy of a whole artificial superstructure of warm clothes and cooked foods.

The slow, inexorable passage south, or southwest, carries on day after day at a steady eleven or twelve knots, a total of perhaps 300 nautical miles on a good day. Almost imperceptibly, hours of daylight increase as you glide towards the Antarctic summer. Voyagers desert the bar for the bridge as twilight lingers on long past its allotted time back in Tasmania.

Various rites of passage are observed and much talked about as though to give structure to a journey otherwise outside the normal constraints of space and time. Some are external: navigation across the Antarctic Convergence, where sea and atmospheric temperatures drop appreciably; passage across the sixtieth parallel which the Treaty defines as the northern limits of Antarctica; passage west across the hundredth meridian – from the Pacific to the Indian Ocean sector.

Others are invented on board by the imaginative expedition leaders to help keep ennui, gluttony and inertia within bounds: a series of afternoon talks by anyone with a tale to tell and perhaps slides to show or a tape to play; an 'iceberg sweep' in which the winner is the person who most accurately predicts the time of the first iceberg sighting (visible by the naked eye and on the ship's radar – no little bergy bits allowed); a chocolate ration which will be handed out to its already bloated recipients "in the bar and only to people with drink in hand". Above all, the much-heralded arrival on board of King Neptune on the day the ship finally crosses the Antarctic Circle.

On the eve of the Neptune confrontation all expeditioners with valid certificates proving beyond peradventure that they had previously been south of the Circle were invited to prostrate themselves (in the bar, drink only temporarily not in hand) before the Voyage Leader and ship's Master while their certificates were examined. Next day, or a continuation of the same day as it seemed to many of the heartier partiers on board, all were ordered to assemble at the fo'c'sle where King Neptune and his Merry Cohorts administered a series of vile rituals for first-time Antarcticans, including dollops of vomit-like soup over the hair and down the neck washed down with ladles of ice-filled water, a blob of almost irremovable red paint on the nose, an excremental potion that had to be drunk – and the donation of a certificate of initiation and welcome to King Neptune's icy kingdom the main value of which seemed to be that you would never again have to be the victim of this humiliating rigmarole. Contrary to rumoured expectation, initiates were not doused by the ship's crane in the freezing ocean, perhaps because by now the waters were already too thick with the broken pack-ice and bergy bits that were to dog our progress and add infinite charm to the view for the next twenty-four hours.

The King Neptune jiggery-pokery marked our true entry into Antarctica, and indeed no sooner had his infamous majesty and court disappeared from the ship and metamorphosed back into the familiar shapes of some of our more experienced shipmates than the hitherto dull southern skies cleared and we were treated to one of those miraculous days that live in the memory. A bright sun shone out through a faultless blue sky over a scene of almost indescribable magnificence. On all sides, sculpted icebergs like giant blocks of ice-cream stood station over our progress, shimmering in the sunlight as we slowly felt our way through the silent seas that lay between. The air was cool, fresh, almost windless, the only motion that of the ship slipping through these southernmost waters of the world. A snowy petrel or albatross would glide alongside, and

Into the Southern Ocean.

once or twice a family of minke whales could be seen breaking the surface, spouting and then curving back below once more.

Gradually, we pressed our way through the broken pack – lumps of flat-topped ice that form the residue of the sea-ice that just a few weeks before would have rendered these waters unnavigable. Our ice-strengthened ship, the *Icebird*, ploughed on through most of the growlers and bergy bits in its path, though by now those steering our path from the bridge had to be constantly vigilant. Our speed was pulled back to eight or nine knots, and voyagers congregated on the fo'c'sle to watch – and listen – as *Icebird* crunched the pack beneath her bows, fully aware that, Siren-like, our icy surrounds could kill as well as thrill. Speed was reduced to seven knots, then six, for the pack was thickening. The grinding beneath the bows was constant now, and the lowering sunlight gleamed blindingly across a flat, glinting horizon. Suddenly we were not alone after all as a little family of Adélie penguins scampered and waddled across a pancake of pack and into the water, leaving footprints and flipper tracks clearly visible. A pair of lazy seals flopped their way across another floe as our ice-crunching juggernaut pushed its way past.

It was cold now and the sun lay low in the sky. A mist began to descend and the icy infinitude took on a pale, ghostly hue:

Adélie penguins not too perturbed by our passage through the pack-ice.

Monument Valley, Arizona, with colour and contrast removed; grey cenotaphs of ice and snow where a few hours earlier stood giant blocks of meringue and ice-cream.

Five knots now, as the brief but treacherous Antarctic twilight settled over us. A mere fifty nautical miles ahead lay the great frozen continent clamped to the bottom of the earth and we had sailed nearly 3,000 to get this far. But, as with air travel, the final descent is often the most dangerous part of the journey.

Something like ninety-eight per cent of the Antarctic continent is covered by a vast dome of ice at places 4,000 metres or more in depth. This ice is not static but finds its way gradually downhill, outwards, in the general direction of the surrounding oceans. The sheer scale of the Antarctic icecap is hard to comprehend. It is getting on for twice the size of the continental United States or Australia and would take several hours to fly over by jet plane. From the more modest height of a helicopter, it is simply a blinding white expanse in every direction as far as the dazzled eye can see. One tries to picture Scott or Amundsen and their teams, tiny specks of black or brown against an unending landscape of white.

In places this stupendous icescape gives relief to the eye by

40

revealing subtle but teasing variations of texture: shadows that hint at a steep incline below; blue ice stabbed by crevasses; a lumpy, ridged surface indicating faster movement towards the ice edge.

Nor does the ice always stop where the land stops. For the great white cliffs that seem to mark the outer edges of the Antarctic continent are often in fact great tongues or shelves of ice stretching out over the ocean. The largest of these – the Ross, Ronne, Filchner or Amery ice shelves – are, in effect, permanently ice-covered seas in their own right whose outer edges crack off during the Austral summer to form the giant tabular icebergs of the Southern Ocean.

Among the most valued parts of the Antarctic land mass to the few humans who venture down there are the least typical two per cent on its outermost fringes that, perhaps because of some freak in the drainage patterns of the local glacier system, remain uncovered by ice. These rocky outcrops of land, rarely more than a few kilometres square, have provided the relatively warm and secure havens sought by the explorers and whalers of old and the scientists of today.

Picture the archetypal Cornish fishing village. A sheltered, horseshoe-shaped harbour overlooked and protected by rocky hills rising steeply above. Along the coast to left and right grassy-topped cliffs zig-zag their way towards infinity. Inland, behind, hills and cliffs rise gently towards distant slopes of smooth grassland; and before you, the sea. Now drop the temperature in your imagination by fully 25°C, cover the sea with ice, transform the gulls to penguins, remove the yachts and cottages, and turn those grass-covered cliffs of chalk or limestone and the sloping hinterland beyond into great walls of frozen blue-veined marble. This is the coastline of Antarctica. Sometimes the ice wall is sheer, a frozen tongue protruding beyond the edge of the continent it covers. Else where its cracks and indentations reveal its vulnerability and in the summer huge chunks of ice cliff break off into the recently melted waters below, scattering seals and penguins, perhaps killing some, while providing fresh sport and sanctuary for others.

There is not much exposed rock on the Antarctic continent, and very few natural harbours on the Cornish model. But one place where all the features occur together is at a spot west of Prydz Bay in what the Australians chose to call Mac Robertson

Australia's Mawson Station with the ice plateau stretching to infinity beyond.

Land after the chocolate manufacturer who helped underwrite expeditions to the region in the 1930s. Here, miraculously, is a tiny coastal area of exposed granite rising out of the sea. Behind and on all landward sides, the ice plateau rises up majestically. And seaward is a deep horseshoe harbour protected by natural arms of rock and capable, when unfrozen during the brief Antarctic summer, of welcoming ocean-going vessels. This is the site of the first of Australia's permanent Antarctic scientific bases and the oldest continually operated station anywhere in Antarctica, named by its founder Phillip Law after the greatest of all Australian Antarcticans: Mawson.

Here, the cottages on the Cornish quayside become transformed into unembellished old container huts strapped firmly on to the uneven rocky surface. Guy lines – essential if the huts are not to be blown bodily out to sea by the raging katabatic winds – constantly trip the unwary. Town planning is rudimentary, though as in Cornwall the buildings are given individual names: not 'Dunrovin' or 'Beechey Cottage', but 'Shackleton', 'Weddell' and 'Ross'. A hut named after Phillip Law contains the old-fashioned 'crapper' (in which urination is not permitted; the functions must be assiduously separrated). Another hut contains the 'OICERY' where the Officer In Charge, or Station Leader, holds court.

42

A little higher up the hill are other buildings, the mess and club room, stores and sleeping accommodation. There are science buildings, power generators, diesel workshops, a met station, all pretty much cheek by jowl, though the more recent buildings are more substantial than the early huts and several are still not completed. Along the west arm of the small harbour, sitting uncomfortably on a slither of ice and snow, is one of the last dog teams in Antarctica, due to leave according to the Madrid Protocol on Antarctic Environmental Protection by April 1994. And beyond the dogs, up on the harbour wall are three brave crosses each guarding a rocky cairn: a constant reminder to all of the dangers of Antarctica.

Mawson Station is a tiny, compact village of no more than sixty or seventy souls in summer and less than half that number in winter. Northwards, out to sea, beyond a handful of little rocky islets that hug the coast lies the vast Southern Ocean, frozen over far beyond the horizon for three-quarters of every year. And behind, to the south, its tongue licking the very edges of the station itself, is the ice plateau.

This, ultimately, is Antarctica. Everything else – the voyage, the icebergs, the wildlife, the rocky islands and outcrops, the human camaraderie – all are but prelude to the dome of ice clamped irremovably over the continent itself. One can be easily misled by appearances. The hills overlooking Mawson Station may look like the Sussex Downs after a winter snow-fall, but as you traverse the plateau, in one of those square-nosed caterpillar-tracked military vehicles made by Hägglunds of Sweden, you can almost imagine falling through the ice, as though there were water beneath. There is not. This ice is not a winter veneer covering green pasture or frozen pond. The only thing that lies below the surface here is more ice, hundreds of metres of it even at the outer edges.

It is the sheer vastness of the undifferentiated vista that impresses most. As in the American prairie states or the Australian outback, the scenery scarcely shifts as the hours pass and you wonder whether you have made any progress. Sky and surface on the icecap blend into a continuum of dazzling whites, blues and greys that invite dark glasses even on a cloudy day and can literally blind when the sun appears. Out here there is no frame of reference, no people, buildings or cars against which to assess scale or distance. A mountaintop or rocky nunatak projecting through the ice may look five

Hägglunds, on Antarctic duty, the horizon barely discernible from the sky.

kilometres away and prove to be fifty.

The icecap has often been likened to the ocean. What looks from a distance to be flat and lack features can prove in close-up to be highly particularised – and dangerous. Like the oceans, the icecap is waved, and can at one and the same time support several wave patterns in conflict so that you will pitch and toss and roll as you ride. Navigation marks are few and welcome: an occasional series of drums or canes on the ice, like buoys, indicating a safe route. Mountains rise and disappear from beneath the surface like islands in an ocean of undulating ice. Above all you are very much at the mercy of the elements and the weather can change dramatically – and fast.

In Antarctica, that which is most beautiful is often also the most dangerous. White, the traditional colour of purity, can presage death. When the winds blow and the snow whips up and merges with the colour of low-lying clouds, white-outs occur when the horizon disappears and all distances look the same. What is deceptive to the driver of a Hägglund can be fatal to the pilot of a Twin Otter to whom the ground and sky lie on a continuum of grey-white glare.

Blue, too, can kill as well as charm as it illuminates yet conceals that greatest of Antarctic hazards: the crevasse. The

44

These crosses at Mawson are a reminder that Antarctica has few safety nets.

icecap may be thick but it is not immobile. As it tugs at its outer edges down towards the ocean, sections of ice push forward with varying degrees of pressure as they pass over uneven ground beneath, and fault lines crack apart. Peer or climb into the jaws of one of these crevasses and you enter a phantasmagorical, jagged world illuminated by brilliant, inky phosphorescent blues, greens and purples.

This is a different Antarctica, vast, forbidding, simpler to comprehend, grander and more daunting than anything encountered on the journey towards it. Up here on the plateau, finally, there are few subtleties to distract the imagination, no wildlife to speak of, no shrubs or mosses, few variations or undulations of texture. Some things change: the sunlight, seasons and temperature for example. The winds can be fierce, more fierce or less fierce. But you are tiptoeing here on to the foothills of a kingdom in which you are unwelcome and to which you are poorly adapted. You do so at your peril.

CHAPTER THREE

Polar People

At the northernmost tip of the entire North American continent where the gradual slope of northern Alaska finally
reaches down to the sea lies Point Barrow, a bowbacked spit of
land lying like a giant, scaly whale athwart the sea-ice and
dividing the Arctic Ocean into what geographically amount to
its American and Russian sectors: to the west of this narrow
spit is the Chukchi Sea, to the east the Beaufort.

The spit is little more than a causeway, perhaps half a mile
wide, covered by black stones halfway along their slow geological journey from rock to sand. Detritus of various kinds
litters the area as though every empty pop can, paper
wrapping or piece of rusty, abandoned machinery from the
Lower 48 had blown north and deposited itself here, the *ne
plus ultra* of the North American continent.

There is more here, too: the exposed bones of untended
Eskimo graves, for example. It is not easy to bury someone under the loose shale, a narrow layer of stone wedged
between Arctic winds of often hurricane force and, just
beneath, a stratum of permafrost a mile deep. Coffins would
often have been placed only inches beneath the thin surface,
and a combination of frozen winds and hungry predators
have long since stripped many of the graves bare of all
but a few indigestible bones. I felt like Hamlet as I contemplated a bank of broken bones and boxes on that bare and
inhospitable promontory; how transient, how insignificant a
single human life could seem when exposed to the relentless
Arctic elements. These bodies, most of them, were buried (if
that is the right word) in 1917, 1920, 1922, when many of the
present-day elders of Barrow were already born. Yet here,
turned hither and yon by the elements and gnawed by wolves
and bears, are the sepulchral remains.

I pressed on towards the ocean, past more graves, the

occasional Arctic flower popping up between the stones indicating the human nutrients lying just beneath the surface. It was early summer, yet the sea-ice was still lolling heavily upon the surface, with here and there a crack indicating an eventual brief summer thaw. Thickly muffled, I wrapped my parka around me as I stared out over the bleak beauty, contemplating that there was no land now between me and the North Pole; nothing, indeed, between me and the coastline of northern Russia since the North Pole itself is but a figment of the romantic and scientific imagination.

Nothing moved in the dark grey ocean except the occasional leads of water trying to free themselves from the thrall of ice that still bore down on them. I looked at the ice bobbing there just out from the shore. Flat and white on the surface, I could clearly see its larger, bluer, colder component beneath water level. If all the surface ice I could see was jogging and jostling for ascendancy, there would be a veritable symphony of jangling bergs beneath the surface.

Local Eskimos had told me that there was a lot else going on beneath that surface. I craned forward to see, innocently perhaps, if I could catch any glimpse of the rich sea life that I knew accompanied the spring break-up. That it was there I had no doubt; you only had to look at the gulls and eiders swooping across the ocean to be sure of that. A seal broke the surface in a splash off the edge of one of the floes, and a dark grey slippery head with big black eyes looked at me – quizzically, like an old Edwardian gentleman. What was I doing here? he seemed to be asking. And, before I could formulate an answer, he slithered down into the icy waters again and was off.

I had approached Point Barrow along its eastern side where it lies against the Beaufort Sea. The spit is only a few hundred metres wide, but I returned along its western shoreline: this was the Chukchi Sea. As I made my way back along the stony beach I came across a couple of Eskimo hunters on their four-wheeler staring out towards the ocean.

"What can you see?"

"Those are seals."

I followed their gaze. Perhaps a couple of miles out, just visible in the frozen fog, were two or three black dots, seals basking on the ice floes.

"We're waiting for them to pop up over here." The men

were equipped with hunting rifles. "This time of year they're all over the shoreline."

"How long will you have to wait?"

"As long as it takes."

The two men squinted into the middle distance. I left them to their vigil, glad I did not have to wait with them, immobile, for what could be hours in that cold, dank mist. Nor did I tell them about my encounter at the top of the spit, at the very northernmost tip of America, a few minutes before.

"Hey, did that ice move?"

The waitress, who was supposed to be serving me, had her eyes fixed far out to sea. When the Beaufort ice off the north Alaska coast breaks up in the spring, the seals begin to appear. Which is why she was excited. She may have been serving me pizza. But what she liked to eat was sealmeat. It was late June and much of the rest of North America was enjoying, or suffering, the kind of midsummer heatwave that had everyone reaching for a cold beer and discussing global warming. Down in Fairbanks, which is placed in mid-Alaska rather as Madrid is placed in mid-Spain in the centre of a vast peninsula and subject to the extremes of a continental climate, they were sweltering in near 90-degree heat.

If Fairbanks is Madrid, Barrow is an isolated hamlet up on the Biscay coast, Gijón perhaps, but without the roads and railways linking it to the rest of the country. Barrow, 350 miles within the Arctic Circle at 71°N, is one of the largest Eskimo communities in North America with some 3,500 inhabitants living in boxed houses, most of them provided by the North Slope Borough government. It is a sprawling community, the eastern section divided from the western by a dusty road that crosses between two stagnant and usually frozen ponds. A further road leads along the coast up towards Point Barrow, past a third complex of buildings, once the centre for US Naval Arctic Research and today a ghost town of Quonset huts and boxes some of which are leased out to Borough research of various kinds. Further on still is a fourth cluster of buildings, a kind of tent city of the Arctic which doubles as a refuge for Barrow's overspill and, in some cases, as a set-off point for Eskimo families when they take off from town for the ice and the tundra in pursuit of their highly prized 'subsistence' diet.

48

As in native villages in many parts of the Arctic rim, you cannot buy liquor in Barrow. You are, however, permitted to bring it in for your own personal consumption. On flights in from Anchorage and Fairbanks there are often people with somewhat excessive loads of booze in tow, and not surprisingly Barrow has a lot of bootleg liquor and a major alcohol problem. The City Mayor told me he was a reformed alcoholic. Many of his citizens are not so lucky.

The town has a squalid look at first glance. Walk along the cold, bleak streets and outside many houses you see a broken-down abandoned car, bloody animal skins lying out to dry, a rusty oilcan or two, and piles of wood casing which once contained a refrigerator, a television set or a washing machine. Cola cans litter the sidewalks, and paper or plastic bags blow along the streets.

"But you can't go anywhere from Barrow," said one city official to me as though by way of partial explanation.

"So?"

"If your car breaks down, think about how you're going to get it fixed. Up here, you either do it yourself or, if it's serious, you use the one guy in town – the only guy for hundreds of miles – and he will charge you an arm and a leg."

There are no crushing yards to recycle metal, none of the remote, hidden garbage plants that shield eye and nose from human detritus in the more sophisticated urban systems down south. If your truck or refrigerator or heating system in Barrow needs serious repairs, parts may have to be flown in from Fairbanks or Anchorage or further afield several weeks later and at great cost – as indeed may the expertise capable of fitting them correctly. A repaired truck or snowmachine in three months' time might, in effect, cost scarcely less than a new one now.

If this is true in Barrow, it is even more obviously the case in some of the smaller towns in Arctic Alaska. In one local tip I saw what looked like entire trucks and vans half submerged in waterlogged village garbage, though even here the chief repository for most people seemed to be the front yard.

"Who knows what use you may want to make of a wheel or a chain or a door one day?" a local resident pointed out. "There are no trees around here. We're way north of the treeline, cut off from the rest of America by the Brooks Range a couple of hundred miles to our south, with no vegetation remotely within grasp except the flat, boggy tundra grass. You want wood for a bookshelf? Or to build a cabin out on the land for hunting? That's what you make it with: bits of old cars and old crates lying around the front yard."

But didn't he find the resulting environment offensive with so much rubbish lying around?

"Nothing rots or corrodes up here," he said. "You can leave metal out of doors for decades and it won't rust because the atmosphere is too cold and too dry. Organic stuff, too, lasts for ages – like the wood we make our houses from. That's why it's okay to leave caribou meat outside for drying."

I tried to look convinced. "Come on," he goaded me. "You mustn't be so obsessive about garbage and stuff. We're just as hygienic up here as you people down south!"

Things were beginning to make sense, though I kept coming back to the great expense of goods and services, largely due to transportation costs over such vast distances. How did a native Eskimo population, living in a remote and isolated village, manage to pay for expensive amenities? Or did they live largely insulated from the supposed benefits, and therefore the high costs, of civilization as transported in from the south? The answer is complex.

In some ways, the Eskimo population of this part of Alaska has eschewed modernity, preferring to retain aspects of a traditional culture that has enabled them to survive in these very harsh climes for centuries. Whaling, for example, is still a major preoccupation in parts of the Arctic rim. Every spring in northwest Alaska when the annual whale hunt occurs, the captain of a successful boat is the toast of the village as he and his men haul their giant catch back to shore. Everyone turns out for the ritual and an orgy of communal happiness breaks out. "I get more honour," one successful captain told me with a wicked grin, "than if I were the Queen of England!"

To many Inupiat Eskimos the whale takes on an almost spiritual significance as the largest component in an overall ecological system, a continuum of interdependent land and life of which man is an integral part and with which he has lived in celebratory harmony since time immemorial. The fact that the whale is killed does not mean that it is considered merely an object for consumption, nor is it hunted, like Moby Dick, in a spirit of hatred or resentment. The reappearance of the great bowhead off the Bering Straits and in the Chukchi

Skidoo racing at an Inuit spring festival.

Sea each spring is a sign that God, or nature, continues to provide, a spring festival comparable to those in other cultures. People talk of harvesting the whale, or caribou or seal, much as elsewhere people talk of harvesting wheat or barley. And there are men and women in Barrow on huge government salaries, quite capable of buying restaurant steak or pizza every night of the week, whose eyes light up at the thought of 'subsistence', or 'country', food. Visit their homes and along with a cup of coffee and some cookies you may be offered a sliver of freshly dried raw fish or caribou, or perhaps that delicacy from the whale skin and blubber known as muktuk.

And if the male members of the household start to reminisce, odds are that talk will soon turn to early whaling experiences, who is the best harpooner in town or how the old skin boats were so much better than the one they used the other day. The bowhead whale is the one they hunt, the 'right' whale. In many whaling communities, the walls in homes and offices display a great curve of bowhead baleen, that combination of bone and filter that enables the whale to separate the nutrients from the vast gulp of water he takes in when he feeds (and which enabled Victorian ladies to wear firm yet flexible corsets); at the main entrance to the North Slope Borough office building in Barrow the first thing you see is a great

Inuit homes at Baker Lake, complete with satellite dish and all-terrain vehicle.

bowhead skull on display.

Not only whalemeat but seal, too, and caribou are staple foods in these parts, better by far, the old-timers will tell you, than the prepacked bacon and frozen hamburgers with all their E-additives that are flown in from the south by the airlines, along with dried milk and kool-aid powders. And of course they are right. There is no doubt that fresh caribou meat will do you more good and will enable you to withstand the rigours of the harsh Arctic climate more effectively than the synthetic goods flown in from another world at absurdly inflated prices. If the early nineteenth-century Arctic explorers had learned from the natives and taken more fresh caribou or sealmeat and relied less on canned goods, they might have had happier tales to tell.

Those same homes that display a great arc of baleen, however, also often contain satellite television and a video machine. Alongside the skins and fish hanging outside the house is the latest Honda snowmachine or fat-wheeled all-terrain vehicle (atv). In one Arctic village, I had a tentative appointment to meet one of the town elders. It seems he was at camp, some eighty to ninety kilometres away, living off fish and meat hunted on the land, but was expected back that evening. His folks would phone me when he got back.

It was midnight when the call came. If it was okay with me, why didn't I come round? It was daylight and did not feel like midnight, so round I went. The old man was full of good cheer and told me he had just had a great couple of weeks. He was sorry to see me so late but had radioed for a bush pilot to pick him up and no one had been available until 10.30 p.m. Here, classically, were the oldest activities pursued with the aid of the newest technologies.

"From Stone Age to Nuclear Age in one generation." This is a commonly repeated cliché about the people of the Far North. There has indeed been a hasty marriage of traditional native cultures with the presumed benefits of modernity, and the speed of change has brought in its wake many problems. The Arctic is full of bright, ambitious youngsters who value a way of life still taught and to some extent exemplified by the elders. "One day I'm hoping to have my own dog team and I'll go hunting, travelling wherever I want," said Robert, a young Canadian Inuk I met in Baker Lake. But first he was about to go south and take up a job with a native pressure group in Ottawa. Wouldn't he be seduced by the wealth, the eggs and bacon, the bright lights and the girls?

"Oh, no," he replied, genuinely shocked. "This is my home, this is my nation. Down there I'm just a nobody. Up here I'm an Inuk!"

Like many Inuit, Robert believes he can bridge two cultures, taking the best the south has to offer and using it to enrich life in the native north. He is planning to change his name officially from Robert to Angelik, the native name his parents gave him at birth, and has no doubt that his destiny is to help lead his own people as they struggle to maintain a way of life that he sees as being under threat. He is realistic enough to recognise the benefits of television, jet planes and fax machines and would not wish to be without them. A purely nomadic, hunting life is, he acknowledges, a thing of the past. "What I want," he told me, "is to combine the best of the old with the best of the new."

A noble aspiration. But not every native northerner is blessed with Robert's combination of intelligence, confidence and good fortune. In many towns and villages around the Arctic rim you are likely to encounter young men and women who, far from feeling enriched by their exposure to two cultures, sense that they have been caught between them, painfully squeezed and bruised.

Traditionally, most native northerners lived a partly nomadic existence, settling for a while in areas where the hunting and fishing were good, or where the caribou or reindeer chose to graze, then moving on. "For the first thirteen years of my life I lived in sod houses, or snow igloos, travelling wherever we needed to go to get fish and seal and caribou," said Anne Hanson, former Deputy Commissioner of Canada's Northwest Territories – another who can clearly bridge two cultures with no great difficulty. "All that is part of my life, my upbringing; it has helped mould the person I am now."

Then, as recently as the 1950s and 1960s in many places, governments all around the Arctic rim tried to congregate their northern native peoples into new settlements. Motives were mixed. Faraway authorities in the south could control their northern territories better if they knew where people were; settlement is a way of asserting political presence. With towns came schools, clinics, churches, stores, factories, Distant Early Warning (DEW-line) defence installations and new forms of employment. But these essentially southern establishments transported to a northern environment also effectively brought an end to nomadic year-round hunting, while government housing separated the generations and also the various domestic functions from each other – much to the regret of many who were ostensibly beneficiaries of these new social services.

"You *kabloona* [white people]," I was told by another Inuk woman I met in Arctic Canada, "you like to isolate your children in separate rooms, and you send them off to schools all day where you don't even know what they're doing. When you have friends round in the evening you order the kids off to bed! We don't do that. We love our children. We prefer to have everyone sleeping in the same big room if we can, and we like to cook and to eat in the same room where we sleep. We don't separate all the bits of life out the way you people do if we can possibly help it."

"I notice that Inuit women carry their babies with them on their back," I offered.

"That's right. We like to keep them very close. Now, the *kabloonas* – they push their kids around in a trolley on wheels – as if they were items from a supermarket!"

A bit of poetic licence there. But she had a point. Modern

54

Western culture does tend to divide functions and age groups in a way that the traditionally more communal native culture, with its emphasis on the extended family, would never normally choose to do. Thus, many young Inuit grow up today in the native settlements of Alaska, Canada and Greenland, conscious that they can no longer emulate the life-style of their elders, nor yet compete successfully with those raised in the sophisticated cities of the south. In many villages around the Arctic rim there are the tell-tale signs of social and psychological dislocation. In Alaska, the incidence of gonorrhoea among native women has risen to something like thirteen times that for the USA as a whole. New sicknesses like diabetes, coronary heart disease, tooth decay, obesity and lung cancer are now widespread among people to whom they were once virtually unknown. In Greenland, the suicide rate among young men increased tenfold between 1969 and 1986.

It is easy, and even fashionable, to lay the blame for this state of affairs on white exploitation and without doubt the Far North has been plundered by the south. But many of the white merchants and missionaries, the doctors and teachers who came up to the Arctic, like those who went out to India or Africa, did so for what they considered the best of motives. How could it be wrong to bring the word of Christ to the heathen, or to inoculate children against measles or take them off to special sanitoria to cure them of tuberculosis? Was it wicked to insist that youngsters be taught to read and write – and to learn the dominant language spoken in the south? Were the introduction of a cash economy, of motor skidoos, processed foods, television and video sets, necessarily the unacceptable face of southern imperialism? Were the outlawing of infanticide or wife-beating subtle ways of imposing southern values upon a northern culture? Of course not. But as so often, even genuinely good intentions can sometimes help pave the road to hell.

In many ways, the native north resembles the Third World where rapid Westernisation has left in its wake much social disruption. And, as in many Third World societies, youngsters in the native north are often tempted to romanticise a traditional way of life rapidly becoming unavailable to them, while at the same time hankering after the sometimes dubious benefits they believe that modern forms of wealth make available. One fourteen-year-old Inuit boy, receiving counselling after a suicide attempt, was asked: "What two things do you think would make you really happy?"

"Going out hunting with my grandfather," he said after careful thought, "and having a house like they have in *Dallas*." Far from bridging two cultures, many northerners feel they are being denied both.

Right around the circumpolar Arctic people will tell you that a traditional, indigenous form of livelihood, based largely on renewable resources (i.e. animals), is being rapidly eroded by the pressures of modernity. Sometimes the erosion is brutal. In parts of western Siberia, mining operations have effectively destroyed the reindeer herds in some places, and local tribespeople have been forced to pick up roots and move elsewhere to survive. In North America, things have been subtler. If the Inuit wish to hunt seal or caribou, or in some cases the whale or polar bear, there are provisions permitting them to do so. But nowadays they first need money – to buy guns and ammunition, snowmobiles and gasoline and portable two-way radio sets. So a traditionally simple, nomadic existence on the land has become integrated into the modern cash economy of the south and thus into a whole nexus of alien requirements and obligations.

In Arctic Scandinavia the complaint is similar. Nils Thomas Utsi was sitting at his computer, building up a database of Sami reindeer herding families, when I called on him in his office in Kautokeino in northern Norway. We joked about the way he was using the latest kind of technology to buttress a traditional and threatened culture.

"Cash is becoming more and more important," he said. "You have to have cash to pay your bills. Anything you want these days you have to buy – and that means borrowing money which in turn means loans, interest rates, mortgages and the rest. Without money you're lost. But cash, and the things it can buy – like this computer – are alien to our way of living. We were brought up to live with nature. Nowadays, we can't afford to live with nature!"

"But many of you still herd reindeer. I have met Sami herdsmen on the hills up here in Finnmark living much as their ancestors did."

"Yes, but you can't get good prices nowadays for reindeer meat. The market for reindeer meat is going down all the time and our young people are losing heart."

56

Back across the top of the world in Arctic Canada I found a somewhat similar story unfolding.

"You can't make ends meet by living off the land."

This was Billy Day, an old Inuit hunter from Inuvik on the MacKenzie delta. As a boy Billy learned from his father how to hunt whale, seal and caribou, and how to trap fox and mink and sell them – and sealskins too – to the white man.

"It was the white Europeans who first came up here and taught our people how to trap and hunt for furs and skins. Up until then we had only caught what we needed for ourselves. So we learned what the Europeans wanted, and they paid us in tokens with which we in turn could buy things from them."

This primitive economy based on barter gradually turned into a cash economy, and by the time Billy was growing up he and his family were out on their trap-lines every day and living on the proceeds of whatever mink and marten furs and sealskins they could sell.

"Then suddenly," said Billy with emphasis, "because of the animal rights people, those same Europeans said they didn't want to buy our skins or furs any more. The bottom tumbled out of the market and that's just ruined our economy.

"I've got two sons and they want to continue to live off the land. But I don't think they'll be able to afford to. What's happened is that the whites set us up in a type of economy that was convenient to them at the time – and now it's not so convenient so they're taking it away from us, robbing us of our livelihood."

This is controversial territory. Few Inuit hunters would now defend the clubbing to death of innocent harp seal pups or the indiscriminate slaughter of polar bears. But the prohibition on the import of all sealskin products into some of the world's wealthier countries, for example, has caused not only severe economic hardship among native communities in the Arctic but a profound crisis of confidence.

"The hunters and trappers were the most respected people in the community," says Gordon Wray, a transplanted Scotsman and long-time resident of Canada's Northwest Territories where, when I met him, he had risen to become Minister of Economic Development.

"All of a sudden, the children of these hunters learned from television that hunting and trapping were wicked and that their fathers and elder brothers were evil people. Can you imagine the confusion this must have caused among families? It was like going to Scotland and telling people it was evil to catch fish or breed animals for beef."

"Animals, heh?"

An old Inuit man, with only a few syllables of English, sidled up to me. He held a bowl of stew containing lumps of boiled caribou meat. With his eyes he indicated the little anteroom over his shoulder from which I had just emerged. "Animals," he snorted again, with a wicked smile, as though keen for me to agree. In the anteroom, sitting on the floor, was a group of Inuit plucking raw ptarmigan from the bone and eating it, their fingers and mouths – and the floor – scarlet with blood. The word 'Eskimo' was originally a pejorative term used by Cree Indians to signify the people up in the Far North who "eat raw meat".

We were in the Elders' Centre in Iqaluit, a town of three or four thousand people on Frobisher Bay in southern Baffin Island. The building had been financed by the Royal Canadian Legion but designed in consultation with the elders themselves as a spacious, modern version of a traditional Eskimo community house: circular, with a lower, igloo-style entry hall, a platform for the community leaders, and anterooms for particular functions associated with womenfolk.

It has been said that you are what you eat. All over the world, people like to consume what is produced locally if they can – lamb in New Zealand, fresh fruit in the English West Country – and it is the same right around the Arctic rim. The whale and the seal, the caribou and reindeer, the polar birds and fish: these are among the foods of the Far North. But, in the Arctic as elsewhere, if you share people's diet you also learn something about the quality of their life, their culture, their identity. "What are we? We are reindeer people!" I was told near the northern tip of Norway by a Sami herdsman as he invited me to sample some dried reindeer meat his wife had just served.

One sunlit night in Arctic Canada, I visited John Avala and his family out in their camp to share the caribou the men had hunted the previous day. We were all huddled into a little wooden shack: John, his wife and assorted children and cousins of various ages and sizes. Outside the dogs howled and the winds swept across the frozen tundra. It was a cosy scene and John was obviously a proud and popular pater-familias.

"When you take a caribou," I suggested, eyeing the huge carcass lying by the doorway, "it must feed you for quite a long time."

"No," answered John. "I've got a lot of friends and family, and my parents – everyone gets a bit."

"So how long would one caribou last you?"

"A day or two!"

The generosity and hospitality of the Inuit are legendary (and used to extend to Inuk men offering their wives to visiting strangers). When John Avala shares his caribou with a large extended family he knows the gesture will be reciprocated. Nobody in an Inuit community will starve so long as somebody has food to share. The idea of private property, that this is my caribou or seal because it was I who caught it, is alien to many native communities. I frequently noted Inuit women pick up their weekly welfare cheque, cash it at the local store – and then share out the proceeds with all the members of their extended family.

John Avala's wife sliced off a piece of raw caribou with her *ulu*, the curved chopping knife traditionally used by Eskimo women, and offered it to me. Everyone was given a slice. Then she squatted down on the ground over a Primus stove, her youngest baby comfortably asleep in the pouch on her back. "Do you like bannock?" she asked me – and proceeded to mix a dough which she fried into a kind of fluffy bread, not unlike pitta or Indian nan. This too was shared out between everyone present, including the baby who by now was awake and wanted to join in the proceedings. I do not know what time of day or night it was. Under the midnight sun there was no real way of knowing.

To John Avala and his large family out there in his do-it-yourself cabin on the tundra, the hunting life was more than just a way of providing everyone with cheap and nutritious food. It was a way of educating the next generation in the virtues of a simple, shared, traditional way of life that was fast disappearing.

Deprive people of their own language, too, and you are on the way down the road towards depriving them of any sense of social cohesion.

59

"Norwegian. Only Norwegian," one Sami herdsman told me when I asked what he had spoken at school. "We couldn't speak Sami at all at school. It was forbidden."

An Inupiat Eskimo woman from Alaska had similar memories.

"They told us when we were at school that we were not to talk our own language. Only English. If they heard us speak our language they would give us the strap."

Today things are different. Suzanne Monteith, an Inuk from the Canadian Far North married to a white man and living in Iqaluit, is completely bilingual in Inuktitut and English and works for the Canadian Broadcasting Corporation where one of her jobs is to broadcast news reports in both languages. How did she manage this during the Gulf War for example?

"The computer spits out this information in English and I grab it and go straight into the studio. I start to read, in English, and then translate chunks of the report into Inuktitut as I go."

"And are there Inuktitut words for things like 'Desert Storm' or 'Scud missile'?" I asked.

Suzanne laughed. "You have to interpret as well as translate, really. I mean you have to explain a Scud missile as a kind of bomb that doesn't have a proper aim and might land anywhere, sort of a 'mindless' bomb as opposed to 'smart' bombs. How do you say 'smart bomb' in Inuktitut? We simply don't have words for things like that. It was all quite a challenge, I can tell you!"

Not many words in Inuktitut, I could see, for types of sand or kinds of bomb. But I asked about the many words that are said to exist in the various Eskimo languages for 'snow'.

"Well, of course," said Suzanne, "you have soft snow, hard snow, crystal snow, flaky snow. And they each have a different purpose and a different use so we give each kind a different name. Suppose for instance you wanted to refer to a certain type of soft snow that's particularly good for melting and making water. Well you wouldn't want to use a long phrase like that every time you wanted to make a cup of tea so you give a name to that particular kind of snow. And then you might want to say to your son: 'Look, my boy, go out and cut up some of that very hard snow which can be carved into blocks for making an igloo.' And you don't want to use such a long sentence so that kind of snow, too, has its own word. And then there's the fluffy snow they warn you about in weather forecasts ... oh, there are so many kinds of snow and so naturally each has a word to describe it."

"Just as, I suppose, in English we have words for all kinds of cars – sedan, saloon, hatchback, sports car – or say that the rain is pouring or showering or drizzling."

"That's right. We don't have names for lots of different kinds of trees because we're above the treeline. But for anything to do with the Arctic weather we have a naturally rich vocabulary. Our life is very dependent on changes in the weather."

"Can someone make sure that all the kids are out of the way!"

It was eleven thirty at night and the pilot of our little Cape Smythe Beechcraft, shirtsleeved in the bright evening sunshine, was about to fly a small group of us from the tiny Alaskan village of Nuiqsut back up to Barrow on the north coast. On board were the North Slope Borough Mayor, Jeslie Kaleak Sr, and most of his executives – the Borough officers in charge of health, housing, business development, fish and wildlife, public safety, his chief legal officer and a representative of the Borough College. If this tiny plane had crashed, the administration of one of the largest municipal areas in the world would have been wiped out.

We had flown out to Nuiqsut earlier in the day for a meeting of the Borough Assembly, the seven-person elected arm of the Borough government. These meetings mostly take place in Barrow, the only community of any size in the Borough; but once in a while Assembly and administration will show the flag in the outlying villages. The main event at Nuiqsut was sandwiched between parties: a great pot-luck meal for the whole village at 5.30 p.m. – and, five hours later, a session of Eskimo drum dancing to bring a long day to a close. Now, as the shadows lengthened and the midnight sun dipped as close to the horizon as it ever does at this time of year, a final outpouring of party spirits burst across the tiny gravel runway as the whole village turned out to say goodbye. Our plane was surrounded by a circle of four-wheel-drive trucks and atv's as everyone bade everyone else farewell. Dust flew as children criss-crossed the gravel on their bikes, weaving in and out of the little huddles of adults. Departure time was said to be no later than 11.00 p.m. though it was a good deal after that that the kissing and handshaking and waving finally subsided and

Mayor Kaleak enters into the spirit of things at Nuiqsut.

we had all climbed on board. And later still before all the kids were off the airfield and we taxied to take-off.

It had been a good day for Mayor Kaleak. Less than a year into his job, following in the shoes of an exceptionally dynamic two-term predecessor, he had not found it easy to make his mark. The North Slope Borough over which he presides is the largest municipal region in America, containing an area of nearly 90,000 square miles. "About the same size as the state of Minnesota," he remarked to me casually. Which is to say, getting on for twice the size of England. "But we only have a population of four to five thousand permanent residents." One can easily imagine the cost of bringing health, housing, education, clean water, police and fire services to a population so scattered. It has been estimated that it costs over $25,000 a year to provide high-school education to each child in the North Slope Borough. When a Borough school sports team plays an out-of-state match, air fares alone can top $1,500 for each participant.

But the Borough has money. Lots of it. Established in 1972 in the wake of the Alaskan oil strike, the North Slope Borough benefits hugely from Prudhoe Bay. It does not get royalties on the oil extracted, though the State of Alaska does. Instead it collects a property tax based on the buildings, facilities and

62

equipment – the entire superstructure – placed there by the companies. The more companies like BP and Arco invest in Prudhoe Bay in other words, whether or not their actual oil revenues increase, the greater the amount of tax collected by the North Slope Borough. When I visited in 1991 shortly after the Gulf War, morale at Prudhoe Bay was high and current revenues to the North Slope Borough were running at some $225 million per annum. Not bad for a resident population of 5,000.

It is a matter of great and justifiable pride among Borough administrators that they have pulled up their region of the world, which the American Dream had hitherto more or less passed by, and provided it with every modern amenity. The Borough, in sometimes uneasy conjunction with its private sector counterpart the Arctic Slope Regional Corporation, has rechannelled its oil revenues into any number of schemes, especially in Barrow itself: schools, hospitals, vans that spray water on to the gravel roads in summer to reduce the dust, a system that brings fresh water into people's homes.

There is without doubt a huge amount of money sloshing around the North Slope Borough, and this has not always been an unmixed benefit. Indeed the sheer opulence of the Borough budget has helped create a dependency culture. Unemployment is high with many people living off welfare, and most with jobs work for the City or Borough governments. It was revealing to note, too, the kinds of concerns expressed by the citizenry to their elected Assembly that night in Nuiqsut. When are you going to get me a better house? Why don't you run your own air service with decent, low fares? My young son needs special dental services only obtainable down in Anchorage and the Borough should fly us there. When will my cost of living allowance rise to keep ahead of inflation?

"They expect the government to provide everything," whispered one Borough official to me. "It's a kind of socialism!" Not, I reflected, quite the American Way.

In the old days of subsistence hunting, a primitive form of basic self-help prevailed: you caught and consumed whatever you could, though even then the Eskimos would frequently share the spoils of a successful catch with a large extended family. But the Puritan ethic and capitalistic free enterprise as understood in the south were alien ideas to a nomadic, hunting community – ideas normally voiced by southern whites who came up here because they wanted something that was not theirs: whales, gold, and now oil.

The oil strike in 1968 was the pivotal event in the modern history of Alaska. The native community in northern Alaska was at first deeply divided. Some resented the incursions of the oil men from the south and the deleterious impact they feared a big industry might have on their traditional way of life and on the caribou herds that migrate through the region. Others, perhaps picking up some of the assertive stance that had been adopted by the black civil rights movement in the Lower 48 during that period, sensed an opportunity: if our lands prove to have great wealth beneath them, they argued, then let us demand our rights and obtain our share.

After much negotiation, the federal government in Washington passed the Alaska Native Claims Settlement Act in December 1971 which brought a carefully calibrated combination of land, money and the promise of future revenues to the native peoples of Alaska and led directly to the formation of the North Slope Borough the following year. By the mid-1970s, revenues from the installations going up in and around Prudhoe Bay began to flow into the coffers of the new Borough, the new schools and hospitals were duly built, the predicted financial scandals occurred, and local people began to expect, then to demand, every kind of facility from their wealthy but beleaguered Borough government. "Our policy now is to try to woo people away from a culture of dependency," said Mayor Kaleak to me, a little ruefully, as we flew back after our memorable outing to Nuiqsut.

It was close to one o'clock in the morning when we finally touched down at Barrow. The Mayor and administration were all safe and in good spirits. Hands were shaken warmly as everyone dispersed to try and grab a few hours' sleep. After such a day I was not yet ready for bed. So I wandered slowly through town towards the ocean edge and sheltered my eyes from the low sun as its rays ricocheted off the ice floes from an angle somewhere beyond the North Pole above Russia. A full hour later I finally headed back across town towards bed. A little group of indefatigable children were still playing in the streets under the permanent sunlight.

Time was when the road south of Murmansk paralleling the railway down through the heartland of the Kola peninsula was

Barrow, long shadows in the sun at 1.00 a.m.

out of bounds to all but the privileged. This, considering the number of defence establishments along the way, usually meant the military. Certainly, few visitors ever found their way to Lovosero, a town of some 3,500 inhabitants deep in the heart of the Kola peninsula.

In the post-*glasnost* era the road is now open; that is to say, you are permitted to make the journey if you wish – and if you have a car (several years' worth of salary) and can find enough petrol. Lovosero is nearly 200 kilometres southeast of Murmansk, a long straight road through forest and scrubland, fairly flat and featureless. Every now and then you catch a glimpse of the railway that parallels the road for the first hundred kilometres before you branch off to the left. You pass the occasional military truck, or perhaps a young couple from an outlying village out for a jaunt on their motorbike and sidecar. But for the most part you have the road, and all the brush and tundra as far as the horizon on either side, to yourself. Not the kind of road on which it would be much fun running out of petrol, and do not expect to buy a roadside drink or snack. Just be grateful you are allowed on this road at all.

It was a warm Sunday in July, and when we reached Lovosero it looked at first as though the town were deserted. Many people were out in the surrounding woodlands picking mush-rooms and berries. Some were visiting family or friends. The balconies of the big concrete apartment blocks were empty. This part of town was built in uniform Soviet grey – just the place to get out of on a warm summer weekend.

But Lovosero is no ordinary village. For this is the heart of Russia's Sami population, the Lappish minority whose ancient language and culture, suppressed under Soviet rule, are beginning to flower once more and give them a sense of identity with native peoples right around the northern rim of the world.

Raisa Kanyova works as a telephonist in the local govern-ment building. A lively, sociable woman in her late forties, she sits in her office by the department's phone and makes sure that everyone who is not actually out of town drops by for a chat. When you talk to Raisa these days you do so if you can, not in Russian, but in Sami.

"It is our language that makes us distinctive," she explained to me through two layers of translation. "The language – and the reindeer culture out of which it developed."

In Stalin's time, especially during the War, Sami culture was all but obliterated in Russia. Many families were removed from the land and the language was virtually proscribed. There was some return to the old ways later on and in the 1950s the few Sami families left lived in a number of tiny villages in the region – when they weren't following the local reindeer herds north to the coast in the summer and back south in the winter. Then in the 1960s Brezhnev had the bright idea of bringing them all together into a single population centre so that the local Reindeer Collective could be more rationally managed. So the Sami herdsmen and their families were themselves herded into a series of great concrete apart-ment blocks that were thrown up alongside the older, picturesque wooden houses, and modern Lovosero was born. Sami reindeer culture was thus, if not exactly prohibited, effectively discouraged to the point of virtual disappearance.

I wondered what chance it had of surviving in Brezhnev-era apartment blocks? And what did the youngsters know or care of the Sami language?

"You are right," Raisa sighed. "What we have here now is in effect a reindeer factory, selling meat, hides and antlers like any other industrial product."

As for the children of Lovosero, several were at that very moment closeted in the Sami House of Culture a hundred metres down the road, seeking solace on a boring Sunday afternoon watching videos. I crept in and glanced up at the screen. What they were watching was Disney cartoons – dubbed not into Sami, but Russian.

I walked further through town and crossed the river. Here, high-rise concrete gave way to the charming wooden structures that had survived from an earlier era. An old man with a peaked cap and huge, dirty beard, his tongue loosened by vodka, told me how things were better in the old days and pointed over his shoulder towards the reindeer factory with undisguised disdain, bloodshot eyes heavenwards. A couple of children played with a dog nearby, while their mother, flare-skirted and headscarfed, sang to herself as she hung up the family washing on the line.

It was an attractive glimpse of a different world and I was in reflective mood when I returned to talk again with Raisa and her friends later in the day. Surely the old tradition of reindeer herding and the Sami culture associated with it were gone for ever?

By now there were a number of people in Raisa's cramped office and my questioning set off a lively debate. Lydia, a pretty young music student home from university for her summer holidays, said that as far as she was concerned she was a Sami before she was anything else. And to prove it, she stood up, pink with embarrassment, and sang a charming song she had learned in Sami. Raisa beamed with approval and joined in the refrain.

Two gnarled, elderly women who had been watching the proceedings in silence now became animated. "Ah," said one, "but you youngsters don't know how we used to sing when we travelled over the tundra with the reindeer." And with that, the other woman, hands gripped tightly and gaze fixed into the middle distance, suddenly launched into a crackly rendition of a song she had neither heard nor sung since her childhood well over half a century before.

It was a moving scene, eloquent testimony to the inability of an unpopular political system to stamp out an affectionately recalled past.

In many places around the Arctic rim governments are now encouraging, or at least permitting, a revival of ethnicity – of the traditional food, clothing, music and above all language of native peoples. In Arctic Canada at a largely Inuit school I heard the national anthem sung in Inuktitut, and went one evening to watch native children learn traditional drum dancing, a skill almost stamped out as pagan and subversive a generation or so ago. Inuktitut is spoken and sung quite openly, too, by the Inuit of Greenland where once Danish was mandatory if you wanted to get on in life.

On the hills of Finnmark, the northernmost province of Norway, many Sami still follow the migration pattern of their reindeer herds, travelling 300 kilometres north in the summer and then back towards the largely Sami towns of Karajok or Kautokeino in the winter. Norwegian and Finnish Sami elders voice doubts about the long-term continuance of this life, however. The prices they can obtain for reindeer meat are falling, and many of the Sami youngsters are tempted to go off to Oslo or Helsinki seeking more lucrative jobs.

But here too there are signs of a culture refusing to die. Twenty years ago, as we have seen, Norwegian schools in Samiland insisted their pupils all speak Norwegian. A dozen years ago the government in Oslo built a power station in Finnmark, the original plans for which had involved flooding thousands of acres of Samiland right on the reindeer migration routes. These kinds of threats, at least, appear to be a thing of the past, and the Sami of Finnmark have even been encouraged to set up a body with a quasi-parliamentary brief. They now have links with other native groups around the Arctic rim, particularly with their kinsfolk across the border with Russia.

So will the youngsters of Lovosero learn to speak the Sami language – the *sine qua non* of cultural revival? "Yes," said Raisa confidently, "we have Sami language teachers who now come here regularly to give lessons."

"Where do they come from?"

"From Norway."

In the circumpolar North foreign aid takes many forms.

CHAPTER FOUR

Boom and Bust on the
Last Frontier

For centuries people have looked to the Arctic for new sources of wealth. In earlier times they would go north and simply take what they wanted – animal furs and pelts, ivory tusks from walrus and narwhal, seal oil, whale blubber, iron ore, coal and of course gold. Back in the 1570s, Martin Frobisher led three expeditions to the bay in Baffin Island that now bears his name, initially in search of the supposed Northwest Passage to the Indies but subsequently to try and consolidate his claim to have found deposits of gold-bearing ore. He came home, loaded with ore and honour, but the supposed gold content of all that rock proved to be a myth.

Frobisher's misadventures with what came to be dubbed 'Fool's Gold' do not seem to have deterred later generations from going north to seek wealth, and the history and mythology of the Arctic rim abounds with stories of fortunes won and lost. Whether it was Russian pelts or Yukon gold, there were rich pickings in the Arctic for those who knew where to go. There still are. Today's prospector may still seek gold or silver, but is more likely to be interested in other metals such as lead or zinc or in locating energy-rich hydrocarbons such as coal, gas or black gold – oil.

There are two ways to reach Prudhoe Bay. The first is by the Dalton Highway, a gravel haul road that runs straight up the state the 400 miles or so from Fairbanks with virtually no amenities *en route*. Anything that needs trucking comes up by road – but you had better tell them you are coming. For this road, largely restricted to essential traffic, debouches unceremoniously into an ugly little service-and-dormitory township outside Prudhoe Bay with the unprepossessing name of Deadhorse. Here basic services are available for you and your car. But do not look for frills in this bleak northern outpost.

Deadhorse is the Last Frontier with something like shipboard discipline grafted on. No boots may be worn in the North Star Inn where I stayed. Beds are narrow and neat, toilets and shower rooms communal. Alcohol is strictly controlled. Breakfast is clean, cool and hygienic and largely help-yourself. In the spacious lounge there is a television, a pool table and magazines. But no rowdyism. Never were Frontier desperadoes so quiet and considerate. You have to be if you are to survive up here. If you can live within the rules everything goes like clockwork. If you cannot you are lost. I met one man, an unemployed miner from Pennsylvania, who had spent ten days (and years of savings) travelling hither and thither throughout the state of Alaska in search of a job. Any job. He had read in the Philadelphia papers how mining and drilling jobs were available up here and his last port of call was Deadhorse. His eyes were red with bitterness as he saw his chances of economic salvation evaporate daily.

The men for whom Deadhorse works best are the hired truckers and diesel mechanics, the construction engineers and power workers who are up on the North Slope to do a job, will be paid well for their labours, and will return home, somewhere south, as soon as it is done.

Most come not by the haul road but by jet plane. For Deadhorse's main claim to fame is its airport. What JFK is to New York, Deadhorse is to Prudhoe Bay. The big oil companies like BP send up several flights a week from Anchorage. Over coffee and a bun on the chartered one-and-a-half-hour flight you might catch up with old buddies, or browse through the Anchorage newspapers as you fly past the South Peak of Mount McKinley, at 20,320 feet the highest in the USA. The plane takes you over the relative flatlands in the middle of the state, up over the peaks of the Brooks Range, then down gently, with the long northwards slope, towards the Beaufort Sea and, a whisker short of it, Deadhorse airport.

A short bus ride and I found myself in the Base Operations Center, or BOC, the social and administrative hub of BP's giant Prudhoe Bay operations. The BOC building complex comprises everything that is needed to keep the enterprise ticking over: sleeping and eating areas, leisure facilities, and administrative offices with all the latest electronic gadgetry. Bedrooms are clean and neat, the dining-room spacious, while sports and recreation facilities include a swimming pool, volleyball and basketball courts, a running track, satellite television and a 167-seat movie theatre. There are full medical facilities on site and a fire service – everything to equip employees to live reasonably comfortably in a remote, small city.

Prudhoe Bay is a company town utterly isolated from the mix of normal daily life. There is nobody old, nobody young, nobody disabled. No gambling, no alcohol, no shops, no neighbours, no roads to or from anywhere else. Many would find this kind of clean, hard-working isolation unbearably arid, with its strictly controlled and routinised rhythms of work and leisure. Not the kind of life to embark upon if you are half of a shaky marriage down in Anchorage or wherever. But many relish the life, not to mention the opportunity to earn well and spend little, and company loyalty is widespread.

"I'm third generation," one reservoir engineer told me, when I asked how long he had been working for BP. "My grandfather and father worked for the company before me – first Pure Oil, then Sinclair which in turn became Sohio and thence BP." A whole strand of oil history flowed through his veins and he told me proudly how, from being in the refining end down in the Lower 48, he had come up to Prudhoe so as to be able to work at what might elsewhere be called the coal face.

For most it is a hi-tech life. Communications officer Marie Jordan is a middle-aged mother of two sons who has worked at Prudhoe Bay since the mid-1970s when the complex was still being built. In northern Alaska, says Marie proudly, they are at the very hub of a wheel that includes Russia, Japan, Canada, the American Lower 48, Britain and Scandinavia. "And we're in touch with them all."

The work rhythm would not suit everybody. "Twelve-hour shifts," Marie tells me – and seeing my jaw sag at the thought adds: "one week on, one week off." Once a week, that is, the company jets her the 700 miles between Anchorage and Deadhorse. Does she like this intensive week-on-week-off twelve-hours-a-day work pattern? "I love it. It gives me time to be with my family twenty-six weeks a year, to fly my plane, see my friends. I'd hate to work every day, week after week. It's great!"

Dave, one of the cooks in the BP kitchens, is on a two-weeks-on-two-weeks-off schedule. "What you have here," he says, "is work, workout and sleep!" And, he adds cryptically: "There's no extracurriculars as far as being in a reality-type situation."

Dave seemed happy in his job and showed no obvious signs of missing his extracurriculars. He was certainly kept on the go. Was that because people in the oil world had big appetites? Did he have a lot of hard-eating customers to feed?

"Well, eating's basically all they have to do when they're off duty. They walk around and pick and eat. So you'll find a lot of guys carrying an extra bit of poundage."

Maybe this is also because people sleep on site. Dave rolls out of bed in the BOC, comes downstairs, and there is his workplace. Does he set foot out of doors at all during his two-week work stints?

"Not normally."

"Don't you get stir crazy?"

"I suppose I would if I thought about it. But you're right. Things here are fairly structured and limited versus anywhere else."

Life for many people in the polar regions, far from being solitary as many outsiders assume, is often intensely sociable. For native inhabitants and visitors alike, for the oil worker at Prudhoe Bay, the engineer on board a Russian ice-breaker or the upper atmosphere physicist or plumber at one of the scientific stations in Antarctica, the problem is often not so much personal isolation as its opposite: the omnipresence of the same limited company not of your own choosing and the almost complete lack of privacy or personal space. Native northerners, living an essentially isolated village life, are accustomed to this; visiting workers often are not.

Only those who are truly sociable, adaptable, amenable and generous-natured can flourish near the Poles. Nobody who takes offence easily or demands his or her rights need apply; nor are the polar regions places in which to seek solace or escape from the social pressures of normal society. For you take yourself with you, and out here your personal qualities, undiluted by the hurly-burly of life elsewhere, tend to become writ large. In the pressurised confines of a polar outpost your inner persona will soon reveal itself. Hence the scattered field huts in the hinterland around Australia's scientific stations in Antarctica: work bases, to be sure, but little escape hatches too

– weekend cottages, if you like, for people needing a break. Hence, too, the importance, to those who manage the personnel at Prudhoe Bay, of the week-on-week-off work rhythm. If you want a happy, productive labour force up on the North Slope, you do not tether them down too closely for too long.

Oil extraction involves a complex series of processes and nobody denies the hazards. Drilling descends to a depth of some 8–9,000 feet down through rock and shale, gravel, sand and silt, the first 2,000 feet of it permafrost. If the drilling process, or the drill pads on the surface, melt the permafrost, much damage could be done to the tundra – while the drilling mechanisms could sink out of control.

Once drilling is completed to the required depth, various gases escape upwards, bringing oil and water with them. Oil does not lie in a pool like water in a well waiting to be drawn to the surface. It is in fact the latest geological form taken by the fossilised remains of minute sea creatures, long since integrated with subterranean rock formations, and at this stage of its existence it tends to be deposited in porous rock, much as droplets of water attach to a sponge. Or, to take another analogy: imagine a child's seaside bucket full of tightly compressed damp sand. There is water in the bucket, but it cannot simply be sucked out. Rather, it has to be pumped or pressured up from its rock bed. At Prudhoe Bay the rock bed has built up strong gases and these provide their own escape pressure once bore holes have been drilled. No Oklahoma-style pump jacks are required here. From each well-head, once a certain depth has been achieved, a number of differently directioned holes will be drilled, each curving its way into a rock area filled with oil, water and hot pressurised gases. As the gases push up the bore, they bring with them quantities of the oil and water.

This mixture of natural gas, water and oil thus rises under its own pressure towards the surface of its particular drill or well-head. Some forty to fifty separate well-heads, each atop a variety of directional bores, are clustered close together on one huge gravel pad. From each pad, hot oil, gas and water are directed along a series of flow-lines to a gathering centre where the various components are brought down to atmospheric pressure. The gas bubbles out and is captured. Then the oil and water are separated, the water (and most of the gas)

73

injected back into the ground whence it came to help maintain pressure levels, and the resulting crude oil sent on its way to Pump Station Number One: the beginning of the Trans-Alaska pipeline, an 800-mile journey south right across the state to the ice-free port of Valdez.

This is a complicated industrial process conducted on a colossal scale. The Prudhoe field produces 1.3 million barrels of oil a day and is believed to contain at least 11.7 billion barrels of recoverable oil and gas-related liquids. There are currently around 900 producing wells with another 200-odd still to be drilled. The whole area constitutes some 350 square miles in a region well above the Arctic Circle where winter temperatures regularly hit −60°F. A visiting astronaut compared Prudhoe Bay to a space capsule: every single item of industrial use or human comfort has to be produced on site (water, fuel, electricity), or trucked or flown in at great expense from the outside world. And all waste products have to be removed. So does all that oil.

The last leg of the journey – that 800-mile pipeline from Prudhoe Bay and the various adjacent oilfields on the North Slope down to Valdez – is in some ways the most hazardous. The pipeline crosses three mountain ranges (the Brooks, Alaska and Chugach mountains) and some thirty sizeable rivers, including the Yukon. Much of the pipeline, particularly in the northern part of the state where it runs over permafrost, is above ground. The oil is about 120°F when it embarks upon its journey south, and when it reaches Valdez four or five days later it is still close to 100°F (37.8°C). So, despite several layers of insulation, the pipeline could risk melting the permafrost if buried below ground and this could cause disruption to the tundra, subsidence, and serious danger of breakage to the pipeline itself. Where it is overground, it is held somewhat loosely, to allow for expansion and contraction, or seismic motion, by a series of H-shaped supports whose piles insulate the structure from the permafrost as far as possible. And the sections of the pipeline run at a slight angle to each other, like a train going through a curving tunnel, to give maximum flexibility in the event of a serious earthquake.

The Trans-Alaska pipeline was a highly controversial project in its early days. Native people and environmental groups feared it could destroy the great caribou herds whose grazing and migration paths it crossed. So its vertical supports hold it

The Trans-Alaska pipeline snaking across the tundra.

at an elevation of between five and ten feet off the ground to permit the caribou uninhibited passage. Oil spills were another fear, while the sheer presence of ground-based heavy machinery – not to mention the 70,000 men needed to construct the pipeline over the years 1969–77 – could hardly fail to have a deleterious effect on the pristine Arctic tundra, some people felt. If the project proved a failure in any of these ways, they argued, its impact would be catastrophic. And if it was a success there would be more pipelines, more construction workers, more disruption to the native life and culture of the Arctic. In the event, most of these fears proved unfounded and even sceptics now tend to acknowledge that the Trans-Alaska pipeline has long since justified itself to oil men and environmentalists alike. Daily, for twenty-four hours a day, 365 days a year, 1.8 million barrels of hot oil pass south from Prudhoe Bay and its adjacent fields to Valdez, monitored by a series of pump stations *en route*. If the pipeline were punctured, by sabotage or earthquake, the pumping system would immediately close off the affected section to minimise the resulting damage.

Prudhoe Bay, like much of the Arctic, is a desert. "Like Tucson, Arizona," I was told with a chuckle by one of the many Deep Southerners I encountered. For much of the year

Dust road over marshy tundra.

the air is too cold to hold much moisture, so precipitation is perhaps fifteen centimetres (six inches) per annum. But if there is little snow, there is a great deal of ice. The water trapped on the tundra above the permafrost, unable either to sink or evaporate, turns to ice during the long Arctic winter, as indeed does the surface of the entire adjacent Beaufort Sea. In this flat, treeless region, winter winds are relentless; add the force of thirty to forty knot winds to temperatures of between −20°F and −60°F and below and you have a pretty inhospitable environment (except, evidently, to the handful of Arctic foxes and lemmings, snowy owls and ravens, and a few of the older or lazier caribou who stay up around Prudhoe Bay all year round).

In this bleak and unwelcoming environment, the workforce is quite small and many are working indoors at highly automated computer terminals, rather as though they were air traffic controllers. The huge BP gathering centres, where the incoming oil is separated from the accompanying water and gas, only need half a dozen people each to run them. Plenty of hard-hat labourers come up to Prudhoe Bay on a casual basis, particularly during the brief summer period, to build new wells and pipelines and maintain old ones. But once the nine-month Arctic winter sets in, much of the hardware looks after itself and the regular week-on-week-off workforce do their hi-tech jobs in the comfort of Prudhoe Bay's air-conditioned, open-plan office buildings.

"I'm controlling the flow of oil from the west side of the Prudhoe field to Pump Station One."

Merlene Chun was a smartly dressed young woman, perhaps in her early thirties. She was sitting at a battery of multi-coloured computer screens which, between them, gave her and her colleagues an overview of how all the BP wellheads were performing. "I'm a production controller. That means I'm assigned a certain number of pads on each of which are perhaps thirty separate wells."

And with that she flashed up on to one of the screens a map of the whole Prudhoe Bay region with the BP pads highlighted. A few more keys were punched and we homed into one particular well pad with its cluster of individual wells.

"So you are speeding up or slowing down the amount of oil coming from each of those separate wells?"

"Right."

"Okay. Let's take one of them. Well 13 for example."

A few more keys were tapped and I saw how Well 13 was tied into a network of more or less lateral drill lines deep below the permafrost. The screen showed that, on a scale of nought to a hundred, Well 13 was performing at a capacity of thirty.

"If I want to increase it to, say, thirty-three, all I have to do is select thirty-three and hit the 'adjust' button." Which she proceeded to do and Well 13 out there on its gravel pad above the Arctic tundra was drawing three per cent more oil.

"So why don't you have them all at ninety-nine?"

"Because if we did that we'd be pulling too hard on the field. Remember, the field is under its own natural pressure. When we open up a bore hole, the gas bursts upwards like the bubbles in a champagne bottle. So if you open the wells up to ninety-nine or a hundred you'd very quickly deplete the reservoir pressure and therefore the production capabilities of the field. If you want some of the champagne tomorrow you mustn't leave the bottle uncapped!"

And how can you tell what pressure is acceptable for which well? This is where the reservoir engineer comes in. Susan Brown, for example, who has a degree in chemical engineering from the University of Wyoming. When she graduated, her husband had a job offer with Arco 2,500 miles north in Prudhoe Bay, Alaska, while Susan got an offer 1,500 miles south in Texas. A typical dilemma for an educated young American couple these days. They decided to come north to Prudhoe Bay and Susan soon landed her job with the rival company BP. Today, like most of her colleagues, she spends much of her time at computer screens or phoning or faxing head office down in Anchorage.

The objective of a reservoir engineer? "To obtain the maximum amount of oil for the minimum amount of gas," was how Susan put it to me. Each well has its own gas:oil:water ratio. In the Arctic winter the amount of natural gas that surfaces is of manageable proportions and can be captured, stored and/or reinjected. During the brief Arctic summer, when ambient daytime temperatures can hover in the 50s°F (10-15°C), gas volumes increase so that oil production necessarily declines. "Prudhoe Bay," its denizens like to say, "was built to run below zero." Which is just as well, because that is what it is most of the time. When it gets really hot, say 60°F or over, wells have to close down.

One person who really does work 'in the field' is Jim de Wilde, BP's Environmental Supervisor. He is out and about every day, whatever the conditions, checking temperatures, monitoring water levels in the rivers that run through the site to the Beaufort Sea, collecting samples of air and earth, reporting on the movement of birds and animals; above all, constantly raising the environmental consciousness of his workmates.

I jumped into Jim's pick-up truck and, as we rattled over the raised gravel spine road, I asked him about the biggest environmental bogey associated with the industry: the danger of oil spills. Everybody remembers the incalculable damage done by the *Exxon Valdez* which, on 24 March 1989, poured eleven million gallons (some 260,000 barrels) of crude oil into the waters of Prince William Sound, eventually contaminating over 1,000 miles of coastline. But it is important, Jim emphasised, to remember that that accident occurred not where the oil is drilled but to a tanker 1,000 miles away transporting it. There have been other oil spills at sea (the *Torrey Canyon* disaster in 1967, the *Amoco Cadiz* in 1978). But no spill of remotely these magnitudes – certainly nothing on the scale of the *Exxon Valdez* – has ever occurred at the point of extraction.

True enough. But I pressed Jim. There must be hazards associated with a field extracting and despatching 1.3 million barrels a day (1.8 million if you include the entire North Slope). His answer was to take me on a tour of his daily round of 'what ifs?'. What if this valve, that flow-line or that module failed? What if this bore burst its cap or that pipeline developed a serious leak? How absorbent are the gravel pads on which the wells are constructed?

We drove along the gravel spine road to a spot where two flow-lines converge. This tricky piece of pipeline engineering occurs next to one of the little rivers that help drain the impervious surface of the slope. In winter it ices up. In May and June, however, it swells enormously as it carries rushing meltwater from the Brooks Range down to the Beaufort Sea, sometimes threatening to wash away roads and even potentially the gravel pads on which the oil wells themselves are situated. These rivers running through the Prudhoe Bay site do not exactly 'irrigate' the surrounding land; that would be too grand a word to describe a desert environment that is cold and dark for much of the year and a topsoil going down no more than a foot or two before hitting impenetrable permafrost. But the rivers do provide some drainage for the marshy tundra, and of course fresh water for the summer wildlife, including the thousands of caribou who continue to migrate up here each summer season. Indeed, as Jim and I drove around Prudhoe Bay that day we had to stop from time to time as caribou chose to mosey across the road, rather like sheep in Devon.

The caribou wandered off, kicking and munching the lichens that were sprouting bravely and briefly on either side of the road, and we pressed on, throwing up a cloud of dust behind us for all the world as though we were down in Texas or Mexico. We arrived at a little river. Here, Jim explained, he was planning a 'boom deployment exercise' in the event that oil were to spill on to water. The first essential would be to contain the spill and prevent the oil flowing out to sea. The technology was the same as was used in the biggest oil spill in history – when Iraq poured eleven million barrels of Kuwaiti oil into the Gulf in 1991. A long boom, shaped like a string of sausages, is deployed on the water surface at an angle that will divert the floating oil to a particular spot on the bank where it

Caribou are able to graze alongside Prudhoe Bay oilfields.

can be more easily recovered. Jim showed me how the speed and direction of the current and effectiveness of the booms themselves could easily be tested by the innocent method of throwing biodegradable orange peel and apple cores into the water. 'Oil spill containment' was never such fun!

There have been problems. One winter, for example, they lost the flame on a flare stack because of a faulty valve so that oil was aspirating out into the air to a height of some seventy-five feet across the tundra and spraying all over the surrounding ice and snow. The remedy, once the flare was rekindled? Some sixty people, each with a shovel, went out day after day for a month, and skimmed an eighth of an inch of oil off the surface of the snow. They gradually formed a vast pile of contaminated snow and ice which was promptly doubled in size by further snow and ice whipped up by winds of hurricane force. Eventually, the whole lot had to be melted down and the oil recovered so that by the time of the summer melt none would find its way on to the tundra or into the rivers or ocean. If all this sounds like environmentalism *ad extremis*, I have to report that the roads and rivers and walk-ways of Prudhoe Bay when I visited appeared to be a lot less contaminated with oil than most of the beaches of the seaside resorts in southern England.

*   *   *

Elsewhere around the Arctic rim, economic development has produced environmental destruction, sometimes on a massive scale. My train from Murmansk chugged its way slowly across the Kola peninsula in Arctic Russia, some seventy degrees and more north, gradually up, northwest, in the direction of the Norwegian border. I was on my way to the mining and smelting town of Nikel. The train takes some nine hours to do the journey though it covers not more than about 200 kilometres. It is a single-track line for much of the way. Every now and then we would arrive at a tiny village station with a double track for trains to pass, and wait for half an hour or so for a rare train from the opposite direction. At Titovka, with its little houses with A-frame roofs to shake off the heavy winter snows, I climbed down from the train and mingled with the others standing on the vacant tracks alongside. The guards (hostesses? porters? waitresses? minders?) from my carriage told me they were Moscow students doing a summer job. They chatted to a group of pimply soldiers who had just joined the train, while an old peasant couple from the village, looking as though they had walked out of a Chagall painting, smiled and waved from the dirt road behind the houses.

There were a number of soldiers on board and I soon saw why. We crawled out of Titovka and towards the dusty grasslands dotted with the occasional birch tree. As the fourteen-carriage train curved its lazy way around the village there suddenly came into view a fleet of forty or fifty military vans no more than a hundred metres from our tracks. Then, in a clearing, I saw piles of scrap metal, entire abandoned trucks and other vehicles, and a compound of crude, somewhat derelict huts surrounded, like the wagon circles of old, by artillery. The entire site was littered with rusty oil drums and pieces of discarded machinery   a torn rubber tyre here, a gnarled railway sleeper there. What I was witnessing was the last gasp, or yawn, of the Cold War, a demoralised military camp occupied by people whose political and professional *raison d'être* had been eroded by the forces of history and whose funding, until recently so lavish, was being constantly cut back by an administration in faraway Moscow that lacked both the will and the finances to maintain a respectable army.

For forty years or more, this region was closed to all but authorised personnel, one of the most highly militarised areas on earth. Now (mid-1991) the Russian need for hard currency was so acute and the political clout of its military authorities so weak that a trainful of ordinary civilians, not to mention foreign journalists like me, could steam past, a hundred metres or so away, free to observe, comment upon, photograph or film. Nothing could more starkly illustrate the demise of the Cold War.

We stopped again. This was the little village of Loastari, a dot – or not even a dot – on the map. Earlier, the girls had put a pop music cassette on the tannoy: muzak to distract us from the tedious and repetitive environment through which we were passing so slowly. Now, as the giant train stopped at the tiny station, the music on board continued to play as everyone dismounted once more for a smoke and a chat. Around us, sporadic birch trees pushed their angular way out of the inhospitable northern soil. We were on the very treeline, where boreal forest (or 'taiga') meets tundra. It is an uncomfortable conjunction, the soil too thin and sandy and the winter cold too intense to permit any but the hardiest trees and shrubs to grow. But if ever there was a forest determined to survive nature at her most inhospitable this was it. Alas, the forest had even worse adversaries to confront, as I was shortly to discover.

From Loastari the train continued to crawl north and west. I do not remember when we saw the first slag heap but gradually we found ourselves steaming alongside evil-smelling man-made mountains that were not just the single hills of rotten mining debris that once besmirched the collieries of eastern Kentucky or south Wales, but long walls of waste, table-topped compounds of steaming chemical slag. We were still a long way from our destination, the mining and smelting towns of Zapolyarnye and Nikel, but already the air outside the train contained clouds of chemicals. Many of the trees beyond the slag were by now slumping, agonised, on their sides like a boxer reeling from a heavy blow.

I stood by an open window and contemplated the dying forest around me. It was a lunar landscape, leafless, lifeless. The aftermath of a nuclear attack they had not told us about, perhaps. The images clustered into a shocked mind unable to comprehend what it beheld. By now the sandy surface was giving way to white rock – just one more hazard for these desperate birch trees to overcome. It must be hard enough for them to grow this far north, through sand, rock and tundra, and to survive the severe Arctic winter. Then to be killed by chemical effluent adds a kind of terminal insult to injury.

Some trees consisted now of no more than one or two collapsed branches lying athwart an upright but twisted trunk: a cross above a stone, standing bravely but wilting over the white rock below. A graveyard for trees. This was the archetypal blasted heath you expect to see when you go to *Macbeth* or *King Lear*.

My nose began to block and my throat to go dry. The Arctic sun continued to gleam red but pale through the chemical fog ahead as our train wove its way slowly around the bleak, rocky hills. There in the distance, looming through the haze, I eventually began to make out the silhouette of tall factory chimneys, each belching smoke into this dead, lunar environment. On one of these grotesque, Dickensian edifices was inscribed a crumbling but still legible date: 1979. This was Zapolyarnye, twin town to nearby Nikel. We stopped and most people got out. This was home. The station and nearby factory were bleak, paint peeling, window-panes bare except for cobwebs, walls crumbling. Cranes, abandoned railway track and other metalwork all looked rusty and beyond repair. In every direction beyond the station and adjacent factory were smouldering tabular mountains of slag dominating a twilight vista utterly devastated by mining and its ancillary processes. And all the while, jolly music continued to reverberate through the now almost empty train as we crawled off again for the final leg of this unforgettable journey.

By now it was ten thirty at night and the Arctic sun continued to penetrate the cloudy chemical haze and throw its low orange light on the eerie devastation through which we passed: a ghost train ploughing through the fields of the dead. I stood once more by an open window, breathing in acrid draughts of sulphuric air that smelt like a newly struck match. If the air was killing the trees, what must it do to the human beings who breathe it?

We approached our final destination, the town of Nikel, a modern (or at least post-war) town built, as its name suggests, to support an important nickel mining and smelting works. By this time the surrounding devastation was total: literally hundreds of thousands of dead trees, now, like the fallen on the fields of the Somme. Or perhaps of battles still to come. The

Dead forest at Nikel.

image of nuclear nightmare sprang again into my mind as I took another reluctant gulp of profoundly contaminated air and wondered what it would be like in Nikel itself. Eventually the train pulled to its final halt.

Nikel (population *circa* 23,000) is the administrative centre of the Pechenga Region, an area with a population of about 60,000 pressed up against the northern borders of Scandinavia. It was not Russians who first mined here but Canadians, who in the late 1930s held a concession from the then owners of this borderland territory, the Finns (to whom it had been ceded by Lenin after World War I). Finland lost control of the area as a result of the Russo–Finnish War of 1939–40 and the German invasion a year later. In 1944 this much-fought-over region returned to Soviet control and it was the Soviets who finally established the mining, smelting and metallurgical industry on a proper footing (the Pechenga Nikel Combinat) and built up the factory towns of Nikel and, a little later, Zapolyarnye.

Pictures from the 1950s and 1960s, on display in the excellent Nikel museum, show a typically ebullient Soviet workforce, smiling for the official photographers. And there was undoubtedly an air of optimism as the Nazi menace and then the worst excesses of Stalinism receded into history and

84

gave way to the dull but endurable bureaucratic bungling of the Khrushchev and Brezhnev eras. There was good money to be made in the Far North; scratch the social surface in Nikel or Zapolyarnye or many another heavy industrial complex around the Soviet Arctic and you will come across many workers who came up from Moscow, Kiev, Tashkent or even further afield, attracted by the high Arctic wages, good schools and other facilities, and the relative absence of street crime and other big city scourges further south.

From the start the nickel works were reasonably productive; nickel is one of the most important non-ferrous metals used for military hardware and the Soviet authorities were doubtless particularly gratified to have it produced here in the Kola peninsula where so much of it would be used. There was, then, money, work and status to be obtained in the region.

Today things have changed somewhat. A thousand miles to the east, around the Arctic rim, lies the giant industrial city of Norilsk, with a population eight times that of Nikel and Zapolyarnye combined. Here, stimulated in part by defence needs during the height of the Cold War, new bodies of sulphur-rich nickel were produced in large quantities, all of which needed smelting and refining. So in the mid-1970s the decision was made to ship crude ore from Norilsk across to Nikel for processing. The result was a massive increase in sulphur emissions from the Nikel smelting works and catastrophe for the environment of much of the Pechenga Region. When I stayed in Nikel, a cloud of acid hung over the town causing dry mouths, blocked noses, damp eyes and unhealthy lungs. Locals complain constantly of asthma, chronic headaches and bronchitis. Nobody has statistics of how many deaths are caused; most workers leave Nikel the moment they retire – and die elsewhere. But at what age and of what causes? It is all too easy to imagine.

The smelting plant dominates the town of Nikel. 'Our Monster' the locals call it with a wry smile. All day and all night it belches thick black and yellow streams of poisonous sulphuric smoke across the town and surrounding hillsides, not only from its crumbling chimney stacks but also leaking out of countless cracks in the windows, walls and roofing: a factory built to depressingly Third World standards. Sometimes when the wind is low or in a certain direction the clouds of poison pass over Nikel and leave it largely unaffected but blow instead towards the Norwegian and Finnish borders.

At first, the Cold War being at its height, the Scandinavians did little by way of protest. Environmentalism was in its infancy, and Oslo and Helsinki – not to mention Moscow – were a long way from the affected area. If a Soviet nuclear submarine entered Norwegian waters it was worth making a fuss; there were good brownie points to be gained in Washington. But not by complaining about wafting clouds of sulphur.

But as the Cold War receded environmental concerns grew and the clouds got worse. When I was travelling through northern Norway in July and August 1991, people everywhere spoke about the poisonous clouds from Nikel, how terrible the situation was and how it had to be stopped. A case of kicking the Russian bear while it was down? Surely poor Russia had enough problems without the rich, clean Norwegians chastising them for environmental shortcomings.

"But you don't know how bad it is," I was told by a member of STOPP DODSSKYENE FRA SOVJET (STOP DEADLY SOVIET CLOUDS), a Norwegian pressure group set up in 1990 and based in the border province of Sør-Varanger. "The factories in Nikel and Zapolyarnye pour out nearly half a million tons of sulphur dioxide a year – three or four times greater than the whole of Norwegian industry put together!"

"And how does this affect you?"

"Lots of ways. For example, the berries and lichens on the Jarfjord mountains, which our reindeer eat, are seriously contaminated. And the steel wires that mark the reindeer grazing grounds are disintegrating."

Trivial concerns? Not to people whose regular diet includes local reindeer meat and whose herds were found to be contaminated a few years earlier in the wake of Chernobyl.

In the streets of Kirkenes, a Norwegian town not far from the Russian border, I met Alexei, a young man from Murmansk who was visiting Norway as a tourist. He was asked to sign a petition being organised by the STOP DEADLY SOVIET CLOUDS people, and willingly did so. How did he feel as a Russian, receiving as it were this critical reception from his Norwegian hosts? His answer was to emphasise how important it was that we should all work together to put an end to a shared problem. He and the Norwegians were talking vigorously in fractured English, and I asked them whether such a conversation could have taken place five years before. "Of course not," laughed Alexei. For a start he would probably not have been wandering abroad chatting like this, and he certainly would not have been talking critically about problems in his own country. In the event, Alexei was, if anything, even more outspoken about the pollution caused by Nikel than the members of the Norwegian pressure group who had called him over to sign their petition.

The entire region around Nikel is a veritable image of hell, the aftermath of a Dantean inferno. Yet there are signs of hope. When the problem began, nobody locally dared raise the subject, even among themselves. One of the results of *glasnost*, however, is that ordinary people in Russia like Alexei have learned to protest openly when things go badly wrong. People in Nikel itself who would never have dared voice their complaints to a visiting foreign journalist in the mid-1980s were, by 1991, positively eager to tell me what they thought about the situation in which they were forced to live.

"We want you in the West to know about Nikel," said the local librarian, Marina, in halting but passionate English. And her words were echoed by Tatyana, a local administrator and wife of a mining engineer, who said that talking frankly to people like me was "one way of putting pressure on our government in Moscow to change things".

Tatyana and her husband are originally from the Ukraine and they came up to Nikel fifteen years ago to make a better life for themselves and their daughter. "We have had a lot of talk, a lot of promises. Now we want action!"

How can things be changed? In the West, factories like those in Nikel and Zapolyarnye would simply be closed down as falling far below minimum standards of safety and hygiene.

"But you can't do that here," one local worker told me, another Ukrainian *émigré*.

"Why not?"

"Because these plants provide the only way of earning a living here. If they were shut down – how would we live?"

He is right. Russia, with its devastating economic problems, could not suddenly find new work in the area to support a population of over 45,000. Apart from which, Russia needs the nickel. Poor countries do not close down economically productive factories just because the workers do not like the conditions.

If salvation is possible it will have to come from abroad. The Russians themselves simply cannot afford to break into the rolling circle of economic productivity and environmental destructiveness. But the Scandinavians can. Motivated by a combination of fear, anger, altruism and enlightened self-interest, they are considering committing millions of dollars into various joint ventures to clean up the environment of the Kola peninsula that they share with the Russians. A Finnish company, Outokumpo, and a Norwegian firm, Elkem, are working with the Pechenga Nikel Combinat to develop a new nickel-smelting process designed to reduce the emission of toxic gases.

Joint ventures to clean up the Kola environment are inevitably part of a larger process. For the Kola peninsula is still, years after the end of the Cold War, massively militarised. So the Scandinavians hope that, by helping the Russians to clean up their shared physical environment, they will also be moving towards a greater reduction in the military might that remains as a vast and unwelcome presence to both sides.

They are doing other things too. When I was in Nikel I met a young woman from Oslo, Helje Solberg, who was spending a few weeks in town giving Norwegian language lessons to a very enthusiastic class of locals in return for free board and lodging. Not the most glamorous of summer jobs, you might think, but generous and eloquent testimony to the open hand of friendship that ordinary people on each side are now so keen to extend to the other.

CHAPTER FIVE

History on Ice

Douglas Mawson, born in Yorkshire and brought up in Australia, first went to Antarctica on Shackleton's 1907 expedition. He showed himself to be a first-class surveyor and geologist and also a young man blessed with tremendous mental and physical stamina. Both qualities – the professional and the personal – were put to the test. Together with two companions Mawson not only reached and identified the position of the South Magnetic Pole but also scaled the mighty Antarctic volcano Mount Erebus and gazed down, fascinated, into the jaws of hell. The Shackleton expedition reached the furthest south any man had ever been at the time and Mawson returned to Australia a seasoned and celebrated Antarctic scientist and explorer at the age of twenty-seven.

In 1911, having turned down an offer to join Scott's expedition to the South Pole, Mawson led his own party south to survey parts of Adélie Land and report on the topography and possible mineral wealth of a vast uncharted region.

They sailed due south in December 1911, the month Amundsen was to reach the South Pole. Mawson's ship the *Aurora*, captained by a tall, gaunt Irishman named John King Davis, reached Antarctica shortly before the new year and Davis navigated carefully along the ice-bound coast as Mawson sought a spot to build a base camp. This they eventually found in early January 1912 in an area Mawson was to name Commonwealth Bay. They brought their stores ashore and bade farewell to the *Aurora* which was to return and pick them up a year later, mid-January 1913.

The main hut was erected in the teeth of sub-zero temperatures exacerbated by fierce katabatic winds shrieking down off the ice plateau, and the team settled in for the winter, and to make their plans for what was to come. Once the winter was over the principal reconnaissance journey was to be

Left: Sir Douglas Mawson. Right: The author with one of the dogs at Mawson Station.

undertaken by Mawson himself and two companions: Belgrave Ninnis and the Swiss-born ski champion Xavier Mertz. In mid-November they finally set off confidently: three men, three sledges and seventeen dogs.

The story of what followed stands as one of the most gripping in the history of polar exploration. Tragedy struck first a month after they set out when Ninnis and his sledge containing the bulk of the food and emergency provisions disappeared with half the dogs down a deep crevasse. Mawson and Mertz were stranded with totally inadequate supplies hundreds of miles from their hut at Commonwealth Bay or any form of help. They realised, with unutterable distaste, that the only way they could ever return alive would be to augment their remaining meagre rations by eating their dogs. What they did not know was that the liver of a husky dog contains accumulations of Vitamin A so heavily concentrated as to be seriously toxic.

Within a few days of forced marches and hauling only one sledge now between them with the help of their diminishing band of starving and terrified dogs, the two men began to experience serious headaches and stomach pains that they attributed (rightly but for the wrong reasons) to their abnormal diet, and they became disoriented.

90

Mawson's hut at Commonwealth Bay.

Nauseated by the nature of their rations, weakened by poison, the two men pushed on. They sucked the bones of their dogs, ate the eyes, tried to seek strength and solace in sleep. Mertz noticed his hair beginning to fall out. Mawson opened his boots and layers of skin came away with them. Desperate, weak, emaciated, the two companions feared they might not survive and Mertz began to talk of the most painless way of meeting death. Mawson did all he could to nurse his sick companion and raise his spirits, but in vain. In early January 1913, Xavier Mertz died.

It is hard to imagine the state of mind in which Douglas Mawson faced his appalling situation: alone on the Antarctic ice plateau, far from help, severely weakened by debilitating illness and with the most meagre rations. Somehow, he cut the remaining sledge in half to reduce the load and with parts of the discarded frame formed a mast and spar to carry a make-shift sail to ease his progress. So Mawson set out alone across the deeply crevassed summer ice, harnessed to his half-sledge, much of his skin – including the soles of his feet – separating from his broken body, still hoping somehow to cover the remaining hundred miles to Commonwealth Bay in time to be rescued by the *Aurora*. At one point he fell into a crevasse, but his little sledge bridged the aperture and somehow this sickly

91

skeleton of a man managed to drag himself back up to the surface.

Finally, unbelievably, Mawson managed to stagger back to the hut in Commonwealth Bay – just in time to see Captain Davis and the *Aurora* steaming away. But they had left a tiny relief party in case he and his two companions should still return. The relief party nursed their emaciated leader slowly back to health and for nearly another year they remained in their windbound hut overlooking Commonwealth Bay until, in December 1913, two years after they had first arrived, the *Aurora* appeared once again and took Mawson and his companions home.

Mawson was later knighted, became a distinguished professor of geology and in 1929–31 was to lead a combined British, Australian and New Zealand expedition to Antarctica. His work in surveying huge areas of the unknown continent still stands as a major contribution to our understanding of Antarctica. Sir Douglas Mawson died in 1958.

Mawson's hut stands in Commonwealth Bay to this day, despite all that the polar elements can pit against it. Great globules of ice block doorways and windows, while the doors themselves, cracked from years of exposure to the harsh climate, pull against insecure hinges.

Mawson's hut, like those of Scott or Shackleton, was built for a purpose which at the time it admirably fulfilled. The owners of these remote edifices gave little thought to any subsequent use to which their huts might be put except perhaps as temporary shelter to successor expeditioners. It is a valued and venerable polar tradition when you move on from a refuge to leave some basic rations, medical supplies and perhaps a sleeping-bag or two for others who might follow you. But essentially, these men built their Antarctic quarters, used them for as long as necessary, and moved on.

Eighty years later and we have become preoccupied with the environment in ways that would have amazed our polar predecessors. When Peary went north or Amundsen south they took dogs. To feed the dogs, and indeed themselves, they killed seals and other locally available meat and since the two regions were so vast and so empty it scarcely seemed to matter what detritus you left there. Early polar camps, like mining camps, tended to be littered with garbage. It would be foolish to judge one generation by the standards of another and absurd to blame Nansen or Shackleton, or more recent explorers like Vivian Fuchs or Phillip Law, for killing and eating seal or penguin or for leaving empty oil drums or wooden crates at abandoned polar campsites. To the polar explorer or scientist it would have seemed unnecessarily fastidious, as recently as the 1960s, to have refused on principle to kill and eat local wildlife – and downright absurd to have gone to the effort and expense of returning every discarded packing case or empty oil drum (let alone human waste) from the vast and remote polar regions to centres of population like Melbourne or London.

By the 1980s, environmental concerns had moved from the fringes of public debate to centre stage, from fad to fashion. Where once the respectable media dismissed with derision those who warned of the dangerous side-effects of chemical pesticides or of over-assiduous sunbathing, the new environmentalists who took up these old cudgels were heeded with greater respect. Asbestos was torn out of otherwise sound buildings and automobiles converted to take lead-free gasoline. Supermarket shoppers sought out products that were biodegradable, polyunsaturated and organic and gravitated towards foods that were free of excessive additives or cholesterol.

Many things contributed to this shift in attitudes, among them the writings of people like Rachel Carson, Paul Ehrlich, Ralph Nader or E. F. Schumacher and the sheer pressure of more people on the planet all wishing to consume their share of the world's finite resources. But two developments in particular, both associated with the polar regions, had a powerful impact upon the popular imagination and helped concentrate minds on the issue of apparent environmental degradation.

The first was the greenhouse effect. The earth's atmosphere, it was said, was getting warmer, apparently as a direct result of gases that we humans were releasing into the earth's atmosphere. The chief culprit appeared to be increased emissions of carbon dioxide released by the burning of fossil fuels like coal and oil.

The theory was this. The energy that comes down to us from the sun arrives at the earth's surface and heats the ground and that in turn warms the lower levels of the atmosphere above the earth. But once that energy has arrived it has to go somewhere – if it just stayed where it was the earth and its atmosphere would simply get warmer and warmer. What actually happens is that energy normally leaves the earth in the form of long-wave infra-red radiation which works its way as heat up from the ground through the earth's atmosphere out into space. As the infra-red energy rises through the earth's atmosphere, however, some of it gets absorbed or slowed down by the gases it encounters, and it is this balance between the infra-red that escapes and that which does not that has normally helped maintain an equable temperature on and immediately above the surface of the earth. Now, one of the gases that tends to absorb or retain rising infra-red radiation is carbon dioxide (the same is true in varying degrees of methane and indeed water vapour), and our emissions of carbon dioxide and other greenhouse gases into the atmosphere appear to have grown considerably in recent years. And the more carbon dioxide or other greenhouse gases there are in the atmosphere the less infra-red radiation escapes into space – and the warmer the earth and its atmosphere will tend to become.

There were sceptics aplenty: some who questioned the effects and others the causes. How can you say the world is getting warmer, asked the former, on just a few readings over a handful of recent years? And if the world *is* getting warmer, asked the latter, can you be so sure it is our fault and not just part of a longer-term natural cycle?

Behind the debates about causality, methodology and evidence, one central question forced itself to the forefront. If the world's atmosphere was getting warmer, for whatever reason and over whatever timescale, what would this do to the polar ice at the two ends of the earth? Might not global warming melt the Greenland and Antarctic icecaps and greatly increase sea levels? In which case, were not low-lying cities and their populations at great risk? The issue is a complex one, as we will see in the next chapter, but the debate about greenhouse warming and its possible effects on polar ice undoubtedly caught the public imagination and helped lead to greater environmental awareness and concern.

The other development that helped place environmental degradation at the centre of public debate was the discovery of the so-called hole in the ozone layer. Just as a certain amount of infra-red radiation needs to be able to leave the earth's atmosphere, so a certain amount of ultra-violet radiation from the sun needs to be kept out if life on earth is to survive in comfort. And one of the principal shields from harmful ultra-violet radiation from the sun is provided by a layer of ozone in the stratosphere about twenty kilometres above the earth's atmosphere. By the mid-1980s, scientists working for the British Antarctic Survey became convinced that this protective layer of ozone was becoming seriously depleted and that this depletion, which was seasonal, was most pronounced each spring and summer above Antarctica. The chief cause, though this was at first more controversial, was believed to be the emissions of chlorofluorocarbons (CFCs) from aerosol spray cans, refrigerants and foam-packaging. As the hole got bigger year by year, and a similar but smaller depletion began to be identified over the Arctic region also, sun-lovers learned of the dangers of prolonged exposure to sunlight. Meteorological maps on Australian television showed how the growing Antarctic ozone hole was now of a size to cover Bondi and even the Gold Coast beaches of Queensland, while skin-cancer doctors reported a sharp upturn in the number of patients.

These two issues – global warming apparently resulting from man's emission of greenhouse gases, and the depletion, especially over Antarctica, of stratospheric ozone – rapidly became matters of intense concern and helped push environmental issues to the top of the international agenda. More, they also brought before a worldwide public the vital importance of the polar regions to the health and safety of the fragile planet earth. No longer were the Arctic and Antarctic faraway places of which most people knew little and cared less; suddenly, they came to the centre of attention, bell-wethers of our own future security.

All this would have amazed and doubtless shocked Scott, Shackleton, Mawson and the rest as they sat in their huts and worked out how best to proceed across the icecap. To them it would have been inconceivable that man's puny activities could have an impact upon the global climate or that what went on there in the polar regions could seriously affect life back home. They felt themselves to be pitting their energy and imagination against an immutable backdrop on which no merely human agency could make any serious impression. As they battled with blizzards and pressed their way across the ice, the polar environment would have seemed essentially a local matter, of intense interest to them while they were there but in no serious way affecting, or being affected by, the mass of mankind thousands of miles away.

There has been another change in public attitudes since the age of the great polar explorers which would also have surprised them. This is in the way we perceive the past. We may be more cynical about our historical heroes than earlier generations and enjoy learning about their human follies and failings; where our grandparents would lament Scott's tragic death on his return from the South Pole, today's polar buff possibly experiences a certain *schadenfreude* reading about misjudgments that contributed to Scott's fate. But in an age of ever more rapid change, the appetite for history is evidently growing and insatiable. The more we destroy, the more we feel the need to conserve. We look at a large, decrepit factory long since past its useful life, Battersea Power Station, perhaps, on the River Thames in the heart of London, and at one and the same time feel inclined to demolish it and replace it with something safer and more aesthetically pleasing – while also wishing to conserve it as a monument to our fast-disappearing industrial history. Here, too, new attitudes have fed back into the ways we perceive the polar regions.

What impact has our new environmentalism had upon activities in the polar regions themselves? And how does it intersect with the more eclectic historical awareness that has also emerged in the last years of the twentieth century? If Battersea Power Station can seem to some an environmental eyesore and to others an historical monument, what of the Canol Trail in the Canadian Arctic? This is a series of camps I visited, across the mountains west of Norman Wells in the Canadian Northwest Territories, that were set up during 1942 and 1943 when the Americans tried to build an oil pipeline across to Alaska from northern Canada in case other supplies were cut off by the Japanese. In the event, the pipeline was not needed and the project abandoned. Half a century later, all that remains is a residue of rusty fuel drums and fireplaces, broken glass, rotting mattresses and twisted ropes and wires lying on the sub-Arctic tundra.

Today the Canol Trail is seen as a poignant footnote to World War II, and a project many feel should be memorialised. Thus, what in the 1960s and 1970s was regarded as the discarded junk of a discontinued project has with the years come to acquire the status of historic relic. A similar shift in attitudes is already perceptible with the end of the Cold War and the question of how to treat the old DEW-line stations that ring North America. Obsolete military hardware that should be removed – or monuments of the 'lest we forget' variety?

What of Antarctica? Here, the issues are sometimes similar but the solutions often likely to be different. Take, for example, the various scientific stations that have sprouted up around Antarctica, some of which have long since passed their sell-by date. The British base at Halley on the eastern edges of the Weddell ice shelf has to be reconstructed at regular intervals because its surface buildings become submerged in snow and crushed into the shifting ice and gradually work their way towards eventual freedom along with all the icebergs in the Southern Ocean. The old American station at Wilkes was acquired by the Australians – along with all the junk the Americans left behind. Should – can – the nations that consider themselves bound by the Antarctic Treaty remove every vestige of their presence once they close or rebuild a base?

Some territories that are geographically Antarctic to all intents and purposes are technically outside the remit of the Treaty. The British island of South Georgia, for example, which is pockmarked with glacial mountains, is south of the Antarctic Convergence. Its fauna and flora are Antarctic though it lies just above the line of 60°S, the defining line of Antarctica according to the Treaty. Along the beaches of South Georgia lie the rusty remains of the great whaling stations built earlier in the century by the Norwegians: crates and vats and flensing instruments that testify to a massive and brutal trade that was concluded only thirty-odd years ago. In one harbour lies the half-submerged hull of a whaling vessel, complete with harpoon gun. As you wander over these dead factory relics and the beaches they still litter you are likely to share the experience with penguins and seals and it is hard not to feel that their habitat should be cleaned up and returned to them. There has in fact been some attempt to do just that, but there is no way so vast a reservoir of rotting scrap metal could realistically be shipped across the world to a new owner. However, Grytviken whaling station, far from being removed, has been deliberately retained as a kind of on-site industrial museum with displays of collected relics in the original Manager's Villa.

Nineteenth-century sealers' pot on Heard Island: detritus or historic artefact?

The South Georgia whaling stations have other historical associations. It was here in 1916 that Ernest Shackleton and his companions appeared, dirty, bearded and unrecognisable, after a desperate 800-mile open boat journey from Elephant Island to obtain relief for their stranded comrades. Shackleton was to die in South Georgia six years later; his grave lies along the shore just beyond Grytviken and a sturdy cross looks out over King Edward Point. In 1982, the old whaling station at Leith, just up the coast, provided the flash point for the Falklands War when an Argentine scrap-metal merchant, with the backing of his government but without the permission of the British, set foot on South Georgia ostensibly to remove some of the rusty remains from Leith harbour.

It is not easy to say what should be done about these whaling stations. Even if one is retained as an industrial museum, the rest are too large, the scrap metal too bulky and distances too great to suggest removing everything. Where to? At whose expense? But simply to leave them rotting *in situ*, while historically apposite in some ways, is ugly and dangerous to the visitor and hazardous to the indigenous wildlife.

Somewhat similar issues are raised on Heard Island, an Australian possession at about the same latitude as South Georgia. Unlike South Georgia, where the Norwegians

Derelict huts on Atlas Cove: historic sites or junk to remove?

introduced a herd of reindeer early in the twentieth century which still flourish, Heard Island is one of those rare places on earth that contains virtually no non-indigenous flora or fauna. The island is shaped a bit like a giant toffee in a cellophane wrapper, its centre dominated by Big Ben, a magnificent glacier-covered volcanic cone of 2,745 metres (9,000 feet) rising sheer out of the ocean, which qualifies it as the highest mountain and only active volcano on Australian sovereign territory. At either end of Big Ben is a narrow spit, one of which, Atlas Cove, was a favourite haunt for nineteenth-century sealers. To this day, huge iron pots used for melting blubber still lie on parts of the cove, rusted with age and overgrown with moss.

Atlas Cove also contains evidence of more recent human activity: a series of derelict, abandoned huts erected by Australian scientific expeditions in the years 1947–55 and by an American survey party in 1969. Today the wind whistles through their ruins, as bits of wood and scrap metal blow around the tiny settlement area and, as in South Georgia, provide a hazard for the local seal and penguin population.

One way of dealing with all this human detritus might seem to be to document clearly everything that exists on the site; then to remove the bulk of what is there and to clean up, conserve and clearly label what is left. This is, of course, more easily (and cheaply) said than done. It is an expensive business shipping conservators and their paraphernalia to remote Antarctic islands and perhaps leaving them there for a period while they do their work. But it is a policy that could satisfy both environmental and historical considerations.

Opinions may vary about the extent to which the material remains on South Georgia or Heard Island are of historical or cultural value, but what to do about them is entirely a matter for the sovereign governments concerned, Britain and Australia. With Mawson's hut on Commonwealth Bay, however, we are on different ground. There can be no doubt whatever of its cultural importance. How do environmental and historical considerations intersect here – and what kinds of options are available to Australia on this remote spot on the coast of Antarctica well within the region covered by the Treaty?

Janet Hughes is an Australian conservator and researcher and is one of the few who has visited Mawson's hut, which still stands bravely in the katabatics that howl down nightly from the icecap. We met in another part of the Antarctic continent, at the Australian scientific station named after Mawson 4,000 kilometres around the coast to the west of Commonwealth Bay. What did she think could be done with Mawson's hut?

"We should do all we can to conserve the exterior of the building for posterity. It is after all an important historic site."

"But how many people will ever get to see it? Wouldn't it be better to ship it carefully back to Australia and perhaps re-erect it as part of a polar museum in a big city like Sydney or Melbourne?"

Janet does not think so. For one thing, the timbers are deeply weathered after eighty-odd years of exposure to the Commonwealth Bay elements. To some extent they seem now to be held together by the blocks of ice that have formed and the mere process of dismantling the hut could possibly do it irreparable harm. "But in any case," Janet emphasises, "the point is to see the hut *in situ*, isolated there on the edges of Antarctica itself where Mawson and his colleagues erected it. Only then do you begin to get the full impact of what they did."

A powerful argument, but one that gives rise to almost as many questions as it answers. Quite apart from the huge expense of trying to conserve a wooden building in an isolated part of Antarctica, what is the point of maintaining an historic shrine that few people ever get to see? If the hut is to stay where it is, perhaps tourist cruises should be organised so as to enable more people to visit and enter the hut. Janet Hughes is guarded. "People should certainly be able to see the hut," she says, "and to understand its historic significance. But I don't think it's feasible for them to be allowed to go inside."

"Why not?"

"Well, for a start, all that accumulated ice may by now have a role in stabilising the building. Indeed, beams and door jambs appear to be held in place by accumulations of ice. Removing it so that people can go inside could therefore do the hut more harm than good and speed its destruction. Then there isn't in any case much there to see."

Mawson's hut is not like Scott's or Shackleton's huts. These are looked after by the New Zealanders, are easily accessible from nearby New Zealand and American bases and contain many artefacts: books, boots, tins of food, scientific implements, tools and so on. But Commonwealth Bay is nowhere near any other Antarctic base and Mawson and his colleagues stripped it before they left. Perhaps, some argue, it should be allowed to atrophy and eventually be blown away by the winds – which can never erase the memory of Mawson's achievements.

If this sounds philistine, consider the controversy over the expedition of the Norwegian Monika Christensen who in 1991 set out for the South Pole with the avowed intention of using the latest radar retrieval techniques to find the tent and Norwegian flag left there by Roald Amundsen in 1911 and return them to permanent display in Norway. A splendid idea, said some. Indeed, the great Norwegian polar ship *Fram* is one of the most popular tourist sites in Oslo. But others said that the flag and the tent and anything else that Amundsen left at the Pole should be allowed to stay there. Nobody, after all, goes hunting for the bodies of Scott and his companions, buried under a cairn of ice and by now presumably drifting at a stately and glacial speed towards the edge of the Ross Ice Shelf.

A wooden hut is, however, different from a buried flag or body and raises environmental as well as historical issues. For some years now all the Antarctic Treaty signatories have been careful to try and remove back to the home country every scrap of wood or paper or metal brought into Antarctica. There is, on the face of it, something almost verging on the absurd in the earnestness with which most of the nations in Antarctica assiduously collect their accumulated rubbish and transport it back over vast distances and at great expense, from an empty region which few ever get to visit, to be disposed of in great centres of population. Phillip Law is on record as saying: "I consider that returning rubbish to Australia from our Antarctic stations is a waste of expeditioners' labour and the taxpayers' money ... The decision to return waste matter of any kind to Australia is an abdication of our responsibilities – just stop thinking about it down south and unload the problem, with the wastes, on the community back in Australia."

To this, environmentalists have a number of responses. Some dumping of waste does undoubtedly still occur, though clandestinely. But almost everybody involved in Antarctica would now agree that the nations of the world should come together in an attempt to preserve at least one region on this overcrowded, overpolluted planet of ours from the irreversible degradation caused by humanity.

There are other arguments too. Scientists contend that Antarctica is a huge natural lab. Polar biologists, for example, will tell you that on land and in the oceans in Antarctica there are fewer species than in more temperate zones, but often in greater numbers (eight or nine million penguins, but only six or seven clearly defined species). Their work, not to mention that of colleagues studying the ozone layer and global warming, would be jeopardised if the pristine conditions in which it was conducted were vitiated.

There is an important psychological element to the new environmentalism too. We were asked to hoover our pockets before going ashore at Heard Island. This caused much hilarity aboard *Icebird*. Shouldn't we also wash our hair, we asked, clean our teeth and scrub our fingernails? And, more seriously, why hoover pockets if we were also landing huts and heavy machinery and a year's food, drink, oil and other supplies for the scientists we were leaving there?

The answer, of course, is that the boot-washing and pocket-hoovering, in addition to being a genuine cleansing operation, was also a useful exercise in environmental consciousness-raising. If you have been asked to go to that much trouble before being permitted to go ashore you will probably be that much more careful not to disturb the wildlife or trample on the fragile lichens and mosses of the island.

On the wharves at Davis and Mawson stations when I visited in 1992 lay crates, boxes and sealed drums filled with human waste all waiting to be loaded on to our ship and 'RTA-ed' – Returned To Australia. But should everything be returned eventually? Including the remains of Mawson's hut? How old, or how culturally significant, does something have to be before the normal environmental rules can be waived?

There is no simple answer to these complex questions. Indeed, the conflict between historical and environmental priorities became the cause of some good-humoured backbiting at one Antarctic base I visited when someone broke a coffee cup. Did the bits constitute an environmental hazard to be RTA-ed? Or should they be retained *in situ* as cultural artefacts? Even that was hard to decide. Meanwhile, Mawson's hut continues to brave the elements of Commonwealth Bay, battered by the winds, perhaps sustained by the ice – and virtually unvisited.

CHAPTER SIX

Ice, Climate and Scientific Serendipity

Ny-Ålesund is about as far north as you can go, certainly in Europe or Asia, and still expect to find the warmth of human company. A dot close to the top left-hand corner of the Norwegian island of Spitsbergen, the largest of the Svalbard islands, Ny-Ålesund is not a native community or a defence or meteorological station. Once a small mining town (and still technically under the control of the King's Bay Coal Company), it is a tiny scientific outpost. Much of the real clout here is exercised by the Norwegian Polar Institute, headquartered in Oslo 2,000 kilometres to the south. Every summer, a handful of scientists come here, live together as on a small college campus or kibbutz, and pursue their often exotic projects in the most spectacular setting. Global warming? Go out on the glaciers and check it out. Oceanography? Outside is the last gasp of the Gulf Stream, as it curves around Spitsbergen to meet the icy waters of the Arctic Ocean. Arctic terns nest here before flying off in September half a world away to the Austral summer, while reindeer wander down from the surrounding hills to forage.

Buildings alternate between traditional Norwegian wooden frame and modern Arctic Quonset, with some imaginative cross-fertilisation between the two. You do not go to Ny-Ålesund unless you are booked into a bed ahead of time, there are no shops to speak of, and food for most people is taken communally and cafeteria-style. This is a predominantly male community with most people aged thirty to forty-five: a kind of graduate research college for tall, tough and healthy scientists.

The range of research conducted in and around this great natural laboratory is impressive. During my visit in August 1991 we had an evening at which a variety of those in residence were invited to give a brief talk about their work in

104

progress. Reports that day covered research on the geology of Svalbard, glaciology, marine biology, a study of permafrost dynamics, two studies of the barnacle geese that live in the vicinity, measurements of tidewater in the adjacent fjord, atmospheric research, remote sensing of the polar environment, work on the breeding habits of Arctic tern and a study of the effect of light on Arctic vegetation. Something like eight or nine nationalities were represented.

The settlement lies alongside the King's Fjord, a great inlet that nestles like a Scottish loch beneath the mountains and glaciers to the east and opens out into the North Atlantic and the Barents Sea to the west. The easterly view from Ny-Ålesund is spectacular. In the middle distance, beyond the fjord, a series of jagged mountain peaks (which is what Spitsbergen means) compete with each other for visibility in the swirling clouds and the dappled rays of permanent summer sunshine. And between the peaks, vast frozen rivers of blue-veined ice, culminating in cliffs that would dwarf those of Dover, stand station over the fjord.

These glaciers, shimmering in the pale summer light, embody both power and fragility, rivers of ice slowly on the march. Kongsvegen, or the King's Way Glacier, is moving forward at a rate of several metres a day, perhaps a kilometre a year. The story is similar elsewhere. In southeast Alaska, for example, or Heard Island in the sub-Antarctic, glaciers are moving even faster towards the sea where, as here at the ice edge in the King's Bay Fjord, great chunks of ice will periodically calve off with a wrenching roar that reverberates for many miles around.

In addition to moving forward and pouring off great deposits of ice, these glaciers are doing something else: they are receding. This too is a worldwide phenomenon. Whether in Prince William Sound in southeast Alaska, the Jakobshavn glacier of Greenland or in the Alps of Europe or in many parts of sub-Antarctica the story is the same: glaciers retreating so that ice is calving off earlier and earlier. It is as though the white cliffs of Dover once projected several miles out to sea, but will be likely a century hence to be holding out the waters of the Channel somewhere in the middle of what is now the county of Kent. In Alaska, tourists visit iceberg-filled lakes (at Portage Glacier south of Anchorage, for example) which just a couple of lifetimes ago were frozen glaciers. And much the same is true in northern Spitsbergen of the King's Fjord.

Each day scientists temporarily based at Ny-Ålesund don survival suits and go out over the icy waters to test the changing environment. Dr Martyn Tranter of the Oceanography Department at the University of Southampton agreed to take me with him. Our little open aluminium boat, nicknamed the 'Ugly Duckling', was a noisy beast as she chugged her way slowly eastwards through the thickening ice of the King's Fjord towards the glacier edge.

"We're doing a CTD test," Martyn explained as his two research students drew samples of water from the fjord. "That stands for conductivity (or salinity), temperature and depth. It'll tell us something about how much fresh water there is on the surface and how far down the fresh water is mixing." An innocent enough academic exercise on the face of it, just the thing to pass the time during a cruise amidst some of the most glorious scenery in the world.

But the implications of Martyn's work could be considerable, for the waters we were testing lay at the very interface of a number of different environmental processes. Firstly, we were at the mixing point between ice and water. In addition, the fjord was itself a mixture of waters from two converging sources: glacier melt and seawater – coming together beneath us, furthermore, in an area where no saltwater penetrated until recent times. Finally, the incoming seawater was itself a product of cold northern currents encountering the warm Gulf Stream lapping its way up and around the Svalbard islands towards the Barents Sea and oblivion.

Martyn navigated our tiny craft gingerly through waters so filled with ice that it was hard at times to be sure which element predominated. There were large, multi-textured icebergs – wonderful to behold and dangerous to approach. A few showed thick stains of black or brown – bergs that had calved off from the base of the glacier, dragging rock surface with them. As I watched, one of the bergs slowly turned over as its centre of gravity shifted – and confirmed what everyone knows but is easy to forget when you are in a little boat: that nine-tenths of an iceberg is concealed beneath the surface of the water. The bigger ones were in a sense no problem; they were simply not to be approached. But the waters around us as we navigated ever closer to the glacier edge became a maelstrom of tiny growlers and bergy bits, themselves jostling and crashing and cracking and breaking up like so many ice-cubes in a billion cocktails.

Glacier meltwater is fresh and seawater is salty. So if you analyse the salinity of a melting fjord over time at various precisely located spots, you can begin to learn something about the rate of glacier melt, about the nutrients in the fjord and about the interaction between ice, climate and the viability of animal and plant life.

Water basically recycles. The surface water warms in the summer and evaporates into clouds, rises above the mountains to a height where the air temperature is too cold to hold it, falls on the mountains as precipitation – which in these high latitudes normally means snow and ice – and replenishes the otherwise receding glaciers. Eventually, these very molecules will find their way towards the glacier edge, calve off as icebergs and, in due course, melt back into water once more. However, the amount of ice that calves off from these Arctic glaciers each summer appears to be greater than the rate of glacier advance caused by additional precipitation in a region that is essentially a desert. And it is this negative balance that causes the glaciers to recede and the surrounding seas and lakes to rise.

By now Martyn's team had collected a number of water samples. "Fresh-water plumes from glacier melt," they explained, "tend to move to the surface, rather like smoke from a chimney, so that we'd expect the top of the water column to be fresher and the bottom more saline. The interesting question is to discover how far down the waters mix and to what densities."

We chugged on, Martyn steering deftly between lumps of ice of varying size. Then, quite suddenly, we reached a virtually impenetrable wall: a straight line across the fjord where the ice lumps had congregated, shoulder to shoulder as it were, to prevent us getting through. This was the result of a wind tunnel, howling down through the mountain valleys, pressing the bergs and growlers into line with almost military precision. We could conceivably have pushed our way with oars, boots and muscle power, through a narrow lead to the slightly more navigable waters beyond. But there was no guarantee that our tiny aluminium craft would be able to get back later.

We stopped the boat and regarded the miraculous icescape around us. A seal flipped his way on to one of the floes, watched us for a while, and plunged back into the waters of the fjord. Bergs of turquoise and cobalt blue stood over us, dwarfing our tiny launch. As we watched, one berg split into two and the larger one began to turn over, rolling back and forth like a water-wheel, seeking a new equilibrium – and revealing dark stains of silt from the glacier base as it completed its graceful head-over-heels.

Martyn Tranter told me he is a lecturer in 'Marine Sedimentary Geochemistry' and that his particular field of research in Spitsbergen was the way various materials are transferred into the fjord – in particular, nutrients. "Nutrients enter the fjord from several sources: first, the underlying Atlantic seawater; then, from the glacier, they enter by way of either snow melt (which provides nitrogen), ground thaw (which provides both nitrogen and phosphorus), or from chemical weathering (which provides silica). I'm interested in finding out how and when these nutrients enter the fjord."

"But what's the mystery?" I asked. "Presumably they do so each spring and summer when the ice breaks into the fjord."

"Yes, but in various stages. When the surface snow melts, the nitrates wash out immediately, so the nitrogen enters first. Only after the snow has begun to melt can the ground begin to thaw, and this might trigger a pulse of phosphorus and nitrate. And then, later still, when there's a lot of meltwater on the glacier surface, the water can penetrate through the ice and flush out existing water at the base of the glacier which will be rich in silica."

"So if I were a bird or fish or a seal in this vicinity, when would I have my biggest feast?"

"Just after the sun has reappeared in the spring. The sun's rays interact with the nutrients we've been talking about to produce a mass of phytoplankton and also cause the ice cover to start breaking up. This is the famous spring bloom, the sudden proliferation of marine algae that triggers the return of every form of Arctic wildlife."

The spring bloom, the essence of Martyn's research interest in Spitsbergen, lies at the base of the entire Arctic food chain. What he and his colleagues are trying to discover is exactly how and when the nutrients are produced that enable the bloom to occur when the sun reappears. For if the nutrients were to fail to materialise properly, the entire Arctic food chain would be placed at risk.

108

"We're trying to identify what kinds of factors might inhibit the regular transference of nutrients to the fjord."

"Like what?"

"Well, just think of the way the ice breaks off from the glacier. It may bring various nutrients with it, but drifting icebergs also make the water more turbid and turbidity makes it harder for sunlight to penetrate the surface."

So the questions facing Martyn and his team are whether, for example, the provision of nutrients via glacier melt outweighs the incidental disadvantage of water turbidity.

There is also an even more fundamental question, one related to the overall hypothesis of global warming. If glaciers are retreating, that is calving off more ice than is being added by precipitation and bringing more basal sediment into the fjord than in earlier times, that may enrich the waters of the fjord with more nutrients than ever before. But might it not also render them increasingly turbid and thus ever more resistant to light penetration? In which case one by-product of global warming might prove to be a decrease in the scale of the spring bloom, with potentially damaging effects upon the entire polar food chain.

The implications of possible global warming underlay the work of another scientist working out of Ny-Ålesund, the glaciologist Dr Julian Dowdeswell of the Scott Polar Research Institute in Cambridge University. What interests him is not so much the waters of the fjord but the layers of sediment beneath. These, he believes, may hold an important key to our understanding of the future climatological pattern of the planet as a whole. Julian Dowdeswell is on the Steering Committee of a European programme examining the Polar North Atlantic Margins (PONAM) – the long-term climatic signal indicated by studies of offshore sediments in and around Svalbard and the Barents Sea–Atlantic region.

The last major Ice Age finally came to an end about 10,000 years ago, Julian explained, and we appear very gradually to be moving towards the next. One way to study ice ages is to travel to the point to which the most recent one receded. But this broad sweep of climatic change is complicated by several shorter-term trends and patterns. For one thing, our interglacial period of relative warmth has been punctuated by Little Ice Ages, one of which seems to have lasted from about the fourteenth century until about only a hundred years or so ago. London or Paris, for example, are warmer than they were in 1850, and glaciers all around the world have been on the retreat for a century. Add to this the evident global warming from man-made causes – increased carbon dioxide emissions for example – and you have an environment apparently susceptible at one and the same time to both long-term cooling and short-term warming.

To a glaciologist like Julian Dowdeswell, a study of the King's Fjord in Spitsbergen can throw up valuable data on each of these tendencies and, perhaps, help contribute to an overall picture of the future climatological trends of the planet as a whole.

The most interesting aspect of Julian's work makes use of the latest in hi-tech: an H-shaped electronic seismic system which floats along behind the boat producing a regular clapping sound. An underwater hydrophone can then pick up the reflection of that sound differentially as it returns from the various strata of sediment on the bed of the fjord and the results are recorded on a continuous trace in the cabin of the boat so that you can see, as on a fever chart, the layers of sediment you are sailing over. Each layer corresponds to the depositing of a certain type of sedimentation and this, Julian explained, should help reveal something of the subtle topographical shifts of the region.

For example, an advancing glacier system would produce more coarse-textured sedimentation; if a sedimentary layer is finer-grained, it would be reasonable to assume that the source of the sediment was further away and that the glacier that produced it, therefore, was in retreat. So, by slicing into the sedimentary layer cake – or, rather, by identifying its layers by means of electronic echo-recording – Julian hopes to provide a key to the understanding of glacial movement and, thereby, of climate change.

The seismic device will, all being well, identify the layers. But only by collecting the stuff itself can the sediment strata be accurately dated. So Julian Dowdeswell, like many polar glaciologists, is also in the business of collecting sediment cores. The deeper you go – and the further from the glacier edge – the further back in time the sediment at the bottom of the core will have been deposited. For the moment, Julian is primarily interested in short-term trends, say the past century, so he will only need cores a metre or so in length. Not too near the glacier edge (where a metre of sediment can be deposited in a matter of twenty years) but in mid-fjord.

Svalbard is one of the most sensitive areas in the world to climate change, because it lies not only at the northern extremity of the Gulf Stream but also at the limit of the depression tracks that come up past Britain, over Iceland then up the north Atlantic. These two systems transfer heat towards the polar region. So small changes in the frequency of depressions and in the transfer of heat in the ocean currents can have a dramatic effect. During the period 1910–20, when meteorological records were first kept in Svalbard, average winter temperatures were some 8°C cooler than today. "That," says Julian, "represents the termination of the 'Little Ice Age' in Svalbard."

"And has this change nothing to do with the greenhouse effect?"

"It's very difficult to separate out the various possible causes of climate change. But the warming on Svalbard looks as though it began well before the recent growth in emissions of greenhouse gases."

Julian, his colleagues and I started out and tested the various hi-tech devices on board and in tow. Arctic terns swooped and whooped, periodically attacking vociferously to make sure that the little scientific launch kept well away from their nests and fledglings. And beyond us lay an awesome icescape of mountain and glacier, apparently immutable, yet whose subtle shifts could reveal some of the key secrets of our planet. To identify the exact locations at which sedimentary records were being read Julian deployed the latest form of the electronically driven Global Positioning System, or GPS, which located the boat and its incoming data to within a radius of twenty-five metres or less. There was an antenna on the roof of the cabin which picked up satellite signals and at any given time there were usually at least three satellites within range. I checked the GPS. We were at precisely 78 degrees, 55 minutes and 49.6 seconds North. And 11 degrees, 55 minutes and 7.0 seconds East.

The GPS is far more accurate than any of the printed maps of Spitsbergen. "If you plot this location on the existing maps, you'd find we were on dry land!" As well as improving on existing mapping, the GPS enables Julian and his colleagues to know the exact location of their sedimentary data and, if they wish, to return to the same spot for further observation a week or a year or a decade later.

"The first phase," Julian told me, as we chugged and clapped our way towards the ice front, "was to undertake a side-scan sonar investigation of the sea floor – a sort of physical profile of the sea bed."

"What were you looking for?"

"Surface ridges, for example. Remember, this fjord not so long ago was filled by a glacier. So the surface ridges mark out its annual retreat as glacier ice calves off and melts, leaving a new ice front to settle down for the winter. This tells us, in the first place, the rate of glacier retreat. Clearly (except for the separate periodic phenomenon of glacier surge), the glaciers of this region have been receding systematically throughout this century."

As the day drew to a close we stood up in our little launch and looked at the great blue-white cliffs of ice perhaps ten kilometres ahead of us. "If we were here a century ago," said Julian, "that wall of ice would have been two or three kilometres closer to us than it is now." Global warming can have no more dramatic illustration.

Fairbanks, Alaska, is a city of perhaps 80,000 in the heart of America's largest state. An old mining town, Fairbanks resembles some of its sister mining cities in Nevada and California 2,500 miles to the south, with its somewhat seedy downtown area surrounded by massively spread out suburbs. In mid-summer, temperatures soar well into the 80s F and to the casual glance the lush greenery surrounding the city can resemble that of Oregon or the state of Washington rather than the Far North. When I was in town a faint haze of smoke from some seventy-odd forest fires hung over the city. But the forests on the banks of the dawdling Tanana and Chena Rivers are not of elm, oak or ash but spruce, birch and Arctic willow, capable of great spurts of growth during the brief period of intensive summer sunlight, and hardy enough to withstand nine months of brutal Arctic winter. There are other signs of where we are too. The 'permafrost house', for example, a home in suburban Fairbanks built directly on the surface soil which thawed the permafrost beneath it and segments of which have consequently sunk into a morass of its own making – turning the whole building into a kind of parody Disneyland house of horror. Tourists to Fairbanks are invited to dredge for gold, cruise in a frontier-style riverboat, visit a musk ox farm and be photographed alongside the Trans-Alaska pipeline.

On the hills north of town lies the extensive campus of the University of Alaska, a long swathe of learning at the western end of which is a tall building housing the university's Geophysical Institute. Like a mediaeval fortress proudly flying its banner of identification, this eight-storey bastion of polar and environmental learning is topped by a huge white satellite receiving dish fully ten metres in diameter that is clearly visible to all who aspire to approach it from the town below. My guide was a brilliant and mercurial German *émigré*, Professor Gunter Weller.

The receiving dish is his special baby. It is pre-programmed to pick up as many as twenty or thirty satellite passes per day and record their data – not just while they are directly above Fairbanks but over a far longer stretch, building up a daily picture that extends over almost the entire Arctic region. Furthermore the system is equipped to handle synthetic aperture radar, or SAR, a technology that enables data to be collected independent of darkness or cloud cover and which can look at the surface of land, sea or ice in great detail. As the various satellites orbit the earth, they bounce a series of radar beams down to the surface and record the returns – which give detailed data about, for example, the precise nature and distribution of sea-ice, geological conditions or vegetation patterns.

The picture produced is very extensive, covering a region some 3,000 kilometres in radius bounded by the North Pole, western North America down to southern Oregon, the Chukchi, Beaufort and Bering seas, the Kamchatka peninsula and well into Siberia. It is also very intensive, having a resolution of as small as ten or fifteen metres so that quite small objects can be picked up. This is real 'spy in the sky' stuff, but for non-military purposes.

This new SAR technology looks set to revolutionise the still somewhat primitive cartography of the Arctic and provide a boon to Arctic shipping and meteorology. But its uses are more extensive than that. Botanists interested in the possibility of growing temperate grains or fruit in northern regions as the climate is said to warm can ballast their researches with detailed and daily vegetation maps, while shipping that encroaches into disputed fisheries anywhere in the entire Arctic

113

rim can now be easily identified. The Alaska SAR facility is linked to a variety of international programmes, using European, Japanese and Canadian satellites, and sharing its data with similar receiving facilities in Tromsø in northern Norway, Kiruna in Sweden and a Canadian station near Ottawa.

I asked Gunter Weller what, of all the things the Alaska SAR facility could do, he considered the most important. "Sea-ice," came the prompt reply. "We can distinguish between freshly frozen ice, annual and multi-year ice – and have developed algorithms that automatically classify the ice types and show them on a map. We can also look at the movement of ice by continuous tracking of the ice edges and ice floes from one satellite orbit to the next."

"And who gets the resulting information?"

"It's of interest to a lot of different people. First, scientists doing fundamental research in a wide variety of disciplines. Then we transmit our data daily by satellite to the Joint Ice Center in Washington, DC which distributes relevant material to commercial users – shipping agencies, off-shore petroleum companies and so on. Our data's of interest to various public and private undertakings right around the entire polar rim."

Nor do Gunter Weller and his colleagues at the Geophysical Institute only think polar, as I discovered when I asked him about the implications of Arctic research for the wider world as a whole.

"The Arctic is in many ways the 'weather kitchen' of the world or at least the northern hemisphere (and remember that most of the planet's largest land masses and by far the majority of its people are north of the equator). But it's not just the daily weather that's cooked up here, so to speak. In addition, this is where many important longer-term climatic patterns are determined, such as annual precipitation or temperature trends around the world."

"So if the earth's atmosphere is getting warmer, the Arctic is where you'd identify the trend?"

"It's not the only place of course. But climatic trends do tend to be amplified at high latitudes."

"Why is that?"

"It's as though the polar regions were acting as a pair of heat sinks, sucking away at the earth's energy from the sun (which is received mostly in the equatorial regions) and helping maintain the temperature equilibrium of the planet as a whole. Any alteration to the composition of the polar regions would therefore have an impact on the rest of the planet."

"For instance?"

"An obvious example is glaciers. If polar glaciers melt, this will affect sea level. And this has in fact been happening at a great rate right here off Alaska. But in addition – and this is the important point – there are various feedback mechanisms at work. For as temperature increases there is less sea-ice and consequently more evaporation – so that the moisture content of the atmosphere also increases. Clouds develop – and there is more precipitation. And with increased precipitation there is more snow and ice accumulating on the glaciers. So that one possible by-product of temperature increase is more ice, not less, on the polar glaciers and indeed on the Greenland and Antarctic icecaps themselves. This model would suggest, therefore, that sea levels are set to drop initially because the increased glacier melt due to global warming is less important than the increase in polar ice due to precipitation. When it gets too warm, however, these trends will reverse again."

So global warming, far from necessarily reducing the amount of ice locked up over continental Antarctica, could, at least in the short term, be having the opposite effect while still tending towards a longer-term rise in sea levels.

"And there's one final reason arising from higher atmospheric temperatures for a rise in sea levels," Gunter Weller added, "so obvious that it's easy to forget: the normal thermal expansion of the oceans. As water gets warmer it expands."

It is not just the glaciers that give the polar regions their impact on the rest of the planet. Gunter Weller described the all-important feedback processes associated with the polar distribution of snow and ice and, in particular, the 'albedo' or reflectivity to incoming solar radiation. As temperatures increase, snow cover on land decreases leaving more areas of dark open ground. This absorbs more solar radiation and reflects back less radiation than white, ice-covered land or sea – so that the overall reflectivity of the surface is correspondingly decreased. But a reduction in ice cover will itself contribute to a rise in surface temperatures, thus helping to produce further melting, more extensive snow-free land surfaces and hence yet further absorption of the sun's radiation. Thus, the process is to some extent self-generating.

Much the same is true of the oceans. As the temperature gets

115

warmer the ice in the Arctic or Antarctic Oceans melts. Now these oceans are reservoirs containing a lot of heat storage so that, as you thin or melt the ice cover, more heat goes up into the atmosphere. As the atmosphere warms up that in turn melts more ice – which frees more heat to rise out of the polar oceans and so on. Here, then, is another positive feedback loop. And it is these feedback loops that provide a major reason why any global change in climate is likely to be amplified in the polar regions. If the temperate latitudes were to experience a mean temperature increase over time of say 2° or 3°C for a doubling of carbon dioxide emissions into the atmosphere, the polar feedback loops mean that the change in the higher latitudes would probably be in the order of 5° or 6°.

As one Canadian polar scientist put it to me succinctly: "This is where you'd know about it first – and worst!"

What is actually happening to global climate and what is the role of the polar regions in whatever changes are taking place? Are the theories of Gunter Weller and his colleagues just a series of hypothetical models? Or is the world – and especially the polar regions – warming up in the way he describes? The answer depends in part upon the timescale you adopt.

In the first place there are a number of natural cycles. At one and the same time we are probably emerging from a Little Ice Age while at the same time moving slowly towards another major Ice Age. Thus, if your timescale begins in (say) 1800, the climate in London or Paris may appear to be warmer, but compared to (say) the year AD 1000, before the Little Ice Age began, it is probably cooler. Go back 20,000 years and it is certainly warmer; go back another 100,000 years and it is cooler. The evidence for climate change, and its apparent cyclicity, comes from several different sciences. Glaciologists extract ice cores from the Greenland and Antarctic icecaps, long fingers of ice whose trapped bubbles of gas can give indicators of changing atmospheric conditions going back thousands of years. But the apparent cyclicity of warmer and cooler eras is reinforced by research in an altogether different discipline – astronomy.

As the earth spins on its polar axis it revolves around the sun on its year-long path. But the model is not a simple one. For a start, the earth's axis tilts at an angle to the sun's rays (which is why the northern summer is the southern winter)

116

and that tilt changes over time in two ways. First, the earth behaves a bit like a spinning top whose handle gyrates in a slow circular motion. Think of the handle as the north-south axis of the earth and you can see how the *direction* of the tilt will change if you wait long enough. Then, if you wait even longer, you will notice that the *amount* of tilt also changes as it nods slowly to and fro.

And there's another variable. The annual path the earth takes around the sun is not a circle but an ellipse, and the elliptical orbit is itself changing over time, getting gradually more circular or more elliptical. So there are three cycles that affect, among other things, the amount of sunlight or solar radiation the polar regions might receive: the circle described by the polar axis, its angle of tilt and the shape of the earth's orbit around the sun.

Now, the axis of rotation – the circle above the spinning top – returns to where it started over a period of about 23,000 years; the angle of tilt of the earth's axis oscillates over a period of some 41,000 years – while the change in the shape of the orbit of the earth around the sun completes its cycle once every 100,000 years. None of these three cycles in itself would necessarily cause ice ages on the surface of the earth, but each clearly affects the amount or distribution of solar radiation the earth receives. And when all three are calculated together it becomes possible to work out the likelihood of recurrent glaciations.

All these calculations were developed independently of the work of other scientists – the people analysing gas bubbles trapped in the Greenland or Antarctic icecaps or the sedimentary record beneath polar lakes and seas. But in recent years, astronomical cycles have been shown to confirm hypotheses developed in these other more earth-bound sciences.

"There are traces of all these cycles in the fossil records of the earth," explained Dr Jon Darius, an astronomer and Research Fellow at London's Science Museum and at University College London, "so for the first time, in the mid-1970s, it was possible to show that the model which was supposed to explain astronomical ice ages really did hold sway." That is to say, the periodicities – the cyclical rhythms at roughly 23,000, 41,000 and 100,000 years – could be discerned in polar ice cores and in the record of sediments recovered from the bed of polar lakes and oceans.

And the result of putting all this research together? Like most scientists, Jon Darius now thinks that, for at least the past several million years, a major Ice Age has occurred, probably simultaneously at both ends of the planet, roughly every 100,000 years, with an interglacial in between of about 10–20,000 years. And we are now in, or slowly emerging from, one of these warmer, interglacial periods.

So, several things are probably going on at once, but at different speeds. In the longer run – the next few thousand years – the planet is likely to get cooler as we gradually approach a new Ice Age. In the more immediate future, however, we seem to be emerging from one of the Little Ice Ages that can occur during interglacials, which is why London is warmer than it was a couple of centuries ago.

But what effect are man-made or anthropogenic influences having on all this? Carbon dioxide emissions from the burning of fossil fuels for example? Many scientists are agreed that there does seem to be a new warming trend superimposed upon the various longer-term natural cycles. Sceptics point to the fact that weather stations are often placed on land near centres of population and that this could skew temperature readings upwards. But Gunter Weller points out that by using a large, regional integrating factor, like the distribution of polar snow and ice, you can learn more about overall climate trends than would ever be revealed by any amount of local data. These large polar data tend to confirm the warming trend, and Gunter Weller is prepared to hypothesise that this does appear to result from anthropogenic (rather than essentially astronomic) causes. Man's activities, his consumption of resources and the waste products ensuing, have always been among the many variables involved in shifting climate patterns. But human transformation of the natural environment may now be reaching a point where it seriously competes with – or could even begin to override – the natural cycles.

Thus, the polar regions are especially important in the study of climate, and for two reasons. First, the distribution of snow and ice gives a broader picture of climatic trends than can easily be garnered at more temperate areas where the signals are 'noisier' and often overlaid with distracting factors. And second, the trends themselves tend to be amplified and therefore more clearly identifiable in the polar regions because of the feedback loops created by the

118

interaction between ice and solar radiation.

At the moment there is about thirty-five cubic kilometres of ice on the surface of the earth. Of this, ninety per cent is in Antarctica, locked away in the immense ice sheet that bears down upon the world's coldest continent. Dr Mark Mabin, from Queensland's James Cook University, is a geomorphologist interested in changes in land forms, particularly as these are affected by movements of glacial ice. I met him in Antarctica (his sixth trip) where he told me he studies the lateral moraines, the piles of rock deposited alongside polar glaciers. From these he is able to learn something of the long-term behaviour of the ice, and thereby of the climatic conditions by which it was formed. Mark Mabin has worked on both the Greenland and Antarctic icecaps, and I asked him whether the two were behaving similarly.

"Not quite. In Greenland, large areas of the periphery of the ice sheet are in the ablation zone, that is they're melting. That certainly doesn't happen on the Antarctic ice sheet. In Antarctica, almost the only way the ice sheet loses mass is by the calving off of icebergs."

The key question, of course, is not so much how, or by how much, the ice sheets lose mass, but the overall balance – whether the loss is being made up by the accumulation of equivalent amounts of ice through precipitation. Mark had been working on the Lambert Glacier. This giant frozen Antarctic river acts as a conduit funnelling ice from the polar plateau down towards the Amery Ice Shelf from which it eventually calves off into the ocean in the form of icebergs. The Lambert Glacier is over 400 kilometres in length, sixty kilometres wide in places, and over one-and-a-half kilometres deep. This is the largest glacial system in the world, and it is moving at a rate of something like 400 metres per annum or over a metre a day. Thus, a colossal volume of ice – thirty-five cubic kilometres each year – is being drawn out from the Antarctic ice plateau. Is it being replaced?

"It would be very hard to be sure," says Mark Mabin, "unless your studies were conducted over a very long timescale."

"How long?"

Mark laughed. "A flake of snow that falls on the Antarctic ice sheet may take 100,000 years before it finally breaks off the edge of the continent as part of a piece of ice and sails away into the Southern Ocean. What's happening at the outer edges of the Lambert Glacier and Amery Ice Shelf is therefore the culmination of a very slow process, in part at least a response to climatic conditions that prevailed a very long time ago."

"So today's climatic conditions – and global warming for example – have little effect on the Antarctic icecap?"

"Well, they can have all sorts of effects. A warmer world might be causing increased snowfall on the seaward edges of Antarctica for example. But the larger glacial systems, certainly, are responding to conditions that prevailed many centuries ago."

"Are they receding like so many of those in the northern hemisphere?"

"At some of the peripheries of Antarctica there is glacial recession," Mark concedes. When our ship called at Heard Island, the resplendent ice-covered volcanic rock in the deep sub-Antarctic reaches of the Indian Ocean, Mark pointed to glaciers that were evidently receding as fast as any in the world. "But on the Antarctic continent itself, there's very little evidence of recession. I don't mean it's not happening, just that the response time on these vast glacial systems is so slow that we can't really tell. Remember, we only set foot on Antarctica for the first time a century ago and we have been studying the continent for a lot less time than that."

"What kind of evidence is available?"

"You can go, for example, to the dry valleys around McMurdo Sound, where the New Zealanders and the Americans have scientific stations today. In the early years of the century Scott and Shackleton and others made their bases here and took photographs of various glaciers. You can go to the same spots today and take very similar photographs. But if you go to parts of the Alps or Alaska and check them against photographs from the beginning of the century you'll often find glacier fronts that have receded out of sight of the camera."

"Why the difference?"

"The Antarctic continent is so much bigger, so much colder, and its response time so much slower. Even the small glaciers around McMurdo Sound are believed to be responding to climatic conditions 3,000 years ago, while a big system like the Lambert Glacier is responding to conditions much further back than that. The smaller glaciers of the northern hemisphere, or of Heard Island for that matter, have a shorter response time — and are operating in an environment considerably warmer to start with."

In general, the ice system of the Antarctic continent is so immense that it seems virtually immune, at least in our lifetimes, from any influence greenhouse gases may currently be having on the environment. But there is one region of Antarctica possibly more vulnerable to present-day climatic change than the rest.

The Antarctic continent is really composed of two separate regions, two systems separated by the Transantarctic Mountains. East Antarctica is bigger, older, higher, colder, with a colossal icecap that goes its own slow way. But West Antarctica, the region south of the Atlantic including the Peninsula, is in effect a series of islands held together by an overarching glacial system that makes it look like a single land mass on the map. This region is a more recent construction, less stable, less cold. And because much of the land of West Antarctica is grounded below sea level, the edges of the West Antarctic ice sheet are predominantly ice shelves which float on the sea. Some scientists suggest that, if sea levels rise in response to global warming, these ice shelves will also be raised and their undersides warmed. The fear is that these delicate shifts could eventually dislodge parts of the West Antarctic ice sheet from its insecure foundations causing it to slip off into the Southern Ocean as a series of massive icebergs. There is enough ice in the West Antarctic ice sheet to raise world sea levels by six metres. Hence the sensational press interest when every now and then a super-large iceberg does calve off from West Antarctica.

Why is there so much more ice in the Antarctic than the Arctic? The obvious answer is that polar ice accumulates on land more densely than on the relatively warm seas of the Far North and that the Antarctic continent is vastly bigger than its only real equivalent in the Arctic, Greenland. But Antarctica has not always been ice-covered, nor has the Antarctic ice sheet always been similar to that which covers it today. Mark Mabin and his colleagues have found wood fragments high up in the Transantarctic Mountains that date back some three million years. Ice and trees at the same time? Or did they alternate?

"Most scientists believe the Antarctic ice sheet has been in existence for at least twenty million years," says Mark. "What

121

seems to have happened is that Antarctic glaciation changed its character about three million years ago. Over the previous twenty or thirty million years the ice sheet would have been what we call a 'warm-based glacial body' which responded very rapidly to climate changes and contained ice much of which was not a lot colder than 0°C. This kind of 'warm' ice was very dynamic, able to flow fast and readily able to mould and modify the landscape – the kind of thing we have in Greenland and elsewhere in the High Arctic today where you see rapid glacial retreat. In those conditions certain forms of vegetation can survive above and alongside the ice, rather as they do today in Alaska or Svalbard."

"And then three million years ago the global climate – or at least the climate in Antarctica – shifted?"

"It seems to have done, or at any rate the nature of the Antarctic icecap appears to have got a lot colder. There are no wood chips discovered from after that kind of date and the continent seems to have become covered by the more solid, permanent 'cold-based glaciation' that we still see today: an icecap that moves much more slowly and is far less responsive to external climate change."

"What would have triggered the change three million years ago from a dynamic warm-based glaciation system in Antarctica to the colder, more permanent icecap of today?"

"Nobody is quite certain and several hypotheses have been put forward. Some scientists like to point to the gradual uplift in the Himalayas for example. The suggestion is that at about that time, three or four million years ago, they would have risen to a point in the cold atmosphere above the earth to have had an impact upon global climate as a whole. Huge new areas of snow-covered territory, so the theory goes, would have reflected back a lot more of the sun's radiation than before so that the sun was effectively prevented from warming the earth's atmosphere as much as before. Another hypothesis concerns the closing of the Panama isthmus. Hitherto, the Pacific and Atlantic Oceans would have been connected. But when the bridge between the North and South American continents gradually linked up above sea level – also about three million years ago – the two oceans presumably became thermally isolated from one another. This would have forced colder Arctic currents from the North Atlantic to extend much further south than before, while also helping to generate the

Gulf Stream that nowadays of course flows exclusively north-wards."

As we have seen, it is impossible to talk about polar ice without turning sooner or later to the possible effects of global warming or cooling upon sea levels. At the height of the last Ice Age 18,000 years ago, it has been calculated that there was some forty-five million cubic kilometres more ice on the surface of the earth than there is now – essentially a reduction in the volume of the earth's oceans of some two to three per cent. Sea levels were perhaps 130 metres lower, Tasmania attached to mainland Australia, Alaska to Siberia. By the end of the Ice Age, perhaps 10,000 years ago, much of this extra ice had melted and sea levels risen accordingly. And the impact of today's apparent warming trend on sea levels? These are notoriously hard to measure with certainty but the evidence seems to be that they have risen since the beginning of the twentieth century at something of the order of a millimetre a year and that one of the principal causes is glacier melt. According to the US National Academy of Sciences, the melting of glaciers in relatively temperate regions, notably southern Alaska and northern British Columbia, accounts for the single biggest source of additional fresh water run-off into the world's oceans – bigger, certainly, than may occur on the margins of the Greenland and Antarctic icecaps.

As with mean global temperature increase, the rise in world sea levels may not sound much: perhaps half a metre since the beginning of the century. But this has added to the erosive power of the oceans on land areas close to sea level. People living on the margins of the Ganges and Brahmaputra deltas in Bangladesh or on the Solomon Islands in the South Pacific stand to have their homes washed away if sea levels rise. In the Mississippi delta area, the Gulf waters have caused subsidence and consequent loss of many square kilometres of land each year.

A rise in sea levels may be the most important hazard resulting from glacier melt, but it is not the only one. The *Titanic* is only the most famous ship to have encountered an unexpected iceberg at an unexpectedly low latitude, but glacier melt and retreat this century have littered certain sea lanes with more icebergs than previous generations of navigators would normally have expected to encounter. Again, the seas around southern Alaska provide a particularly dramatic case in point. The scale and rapidity of glacier retreat in the region has littered the Gulf of Alaska and the waters of Prince William Sound with icebergs – precisely at a time when these waters have become a prime conduit for oil tankers. The human and environmental dangers of this combination of circumstances can scarcely be exaggerated. The record of the *Exxon Valdez* oil spill suggests that at one point the tanker requested permission to move out of its normal outbound shipping lane and move east to the inbound lane because of icebergs that were drifting from Columbia Glacier and approaching the westbound lane. A century ago, these waters provided relatively plain sailing; today they can be among the most hazardous.

Let us return to earth. If the study of polar ice and water suggests a recent warming trend, how would that manifest itself on land? Partly by reduced ice cover, and there is some evidence of increased ice-free rock surfaces on the fringes of Greenland and Antarctica for instance.

But there is intriguing evidence of a different kind from a study of polar vegetation. In Alaska, biologists are finding that certain forms of vegetation normally found only below the Arctic treeline are apparently migrating northwards. Some even talk of Alaska as the future bread-basket of North America.

Hardly. There is agriculture in Alaska, as in Finnmark and Siberia, and I have eaten some splendid (and enormous) cabbages and even strawberries produced in the fields (and greenhouses) of the Far North. But systematic arable farming requires recurrent light as well as warmth, and in the Arctic the growing season is simply too short and concentrated for most species to be able to flourish. And this will not change until and unless the tilt of the earth's axis towards the sun edges closer towards the vertical.

So there is unlikely to be a corn-belt in Alaska or a proliferation of apple trees in Siberia. But let us move from a dubious future to a possibly detectable past. What sort of vegetation used to flourish in the Arctic? If we can find answers to this kind of question we have another major clue to patterns of climate change, long-term patterns that might place our own short-term shifts into a broader perspective.

Michael Retelle is Professor of Geology at Bates College, Maine. He works with a team that extracts and examines lake sediments from the High Arctic. Unlike Julian Dowdeswell, for example, who is chiefly interested in short-term shifts, Mike Retelle and his team are after long-term trends.

"We hope to try to reconstruct climate history from layers of sediment much as you might from the analysis of tree rings. If you can reconstruct the long-term climatic patterns of the past," he says, "you get a far better idea of where we are today and where we may be heading."

We happened to catch the same flight one day up to Resolute Bay on Cornwallis Island, part of the Canadian Arctic archipelago. As Mike and I sat in air-conditioned comfort, sipping beers and munching nuts, high above the ice-bound waters of the Northwest Passage, he described how he and his colleagues insert vertical cylinders a metre or more into the lake bed and extract columns of sediment. As in the King's Fjord in Spitsbergen, sediment is principally deposited by the melting of glacier ice. Each layer represents one year's deposit, resulting from that year's glacier melt. But the layers are not of uniform thickness; a thicker layer one year might indicate more precipitation, heavier glacier melt or merely local turbulence on the lake bed. In relatively warmer latitudes, or warmer periods in high latitudes, more vegetation grows, precipitation tends to increase and glacier melt is accelerated so that more sediment is likely to be deposited. And all these deposits, thick and thin, contain some indication of climatic history.

None of this would mean much to Mike and his team unless they could be reasonably confident of the age of their sedimentary strata. Counting the layers can give a rough idea of age, at least back through recent decades or centuries. But in the highest and coldest latitudes, where summer melting is minimal but the layers are well preserved, a column one metre in height can contain sedimentary layers containing clues to climate history going back literally thousands of years. So there comes a point when assessing the age of layers of sediment clearly requires more scientific confirmation than merely counting them.

Various dating techniques have been developed: lead-210 dating, at least for recent times – and for the most distant periods going back many thousands of years, carbon-14.

Carbon-14 is an isotope of carbon which decays. It has a well-established half-life and it is a relatively simple exercise to measure how much carbon-14 is in the organic material you are examining and that will tell you when that organic material was formed.

Mike Retelle has at his fingertips a record, through analysis of sedimentary layers on the floor of Arctic lakes, of climate trends going back many thousands of years, and these tend to confirm the trends identified by scientists using other methods. "It seems that we are in an interglacial period that began 18–20,000 years ago when the ice began to retreat," he says, "and which was at its warmest 8–10,000 years ago. Since then we appear to have been heading slowly towards another major glaciation but this process has been periodically accelerated or impeded by smaller-scale periods of unusual cold or warmth." Mike quotes, as examples, the warming trend around the eleventh to the fourteenth centuries AD and again in our own time, and the Little Ice Age that lasted for some centuries in between.

And there is another kind of insight that Mike Retelle's researches reveal. "The Arctic today," he suggests, "gives you a snapshot of what mid-latitudes would have been like during the last Ice Age."

I glanced out of the plane window at the Canadian islands beneath us, gleaming frozen in the Arctic light, and tried to picture this as mid-summer Detroit, Derbyshire or Denmark 20,000 years ago. As I did so I began to realise that, just as Arctic lake sediments can help reveal the climate history of the Far North, so other aspects of the Arctic environment – such as the frozen tundra 35,000 feet beneath me – have much to teach us about conditions long ago in other parts of the globe. That sparse ice-covered moss and lichen I was glancing at, for example, probably mirrors vegetation patterns common in mid-latitudes during the last Ice Age. Indeed, the very way the topography of the Arctic is gradually being transformed by glacier melt suggests important parallels with what we now think of as familiar land shapes and river systems lower down the map.

As our plane gradually descended towards the tiny outpost of Resolute Bay, I reflected on what Mike Retelle had told me and tried to imagine that our impossibly futuristic aircraft was somehow landing me in the last Ice Age 20,000 years or more ago alongside the frozen estuary of the Thames. In Resolute itself, I was to meet someone who could take me back further still.

Resolute Bay is a small Arctic settlement (resident population: *circa* 165) at 75°N dating back no more than thirty-odd years. Yet it is large enough to have two distinct areas: a largely Inuit settlement, and a separate scientific community some six kilometres away living and working near the airport, the meteorological station and the offices and labs of the Canadian Polar Continental Shelf Project. It was here that I met Roger King of the University of Western Ontario, who is also interested in Arctic lake sediments. What stories does he tease out of his sediment cores?

"They tell you about vegetational changes, about soil erosion, and from this kind of information you can infer data about climate change."

"Over what kind of timescale?"

"About 40,000 years. Up here, decomposition is very slow because of the extremely low temperatures. So we have sedimentary records that are not only more complete and accurate than at lower latitudes but also far better preserved over a much longer time period. Forty thousand years takes you right back through the last major Ice Age (which peaked about 20,000 years ago) well into the warmer period that preceded it and which roughly parallels the interglacial we are going through now."

"How close are the parallels?"

"Well, of course, as soon as you compare sediments from 40,000 years ago and those from, say, the past century or two, even though in both cases we might be presumed to be approaching a period of glaciation, certain important differences appear. For example, sedimentary strata from a couple of hundred years ago reveal changes in atmospheric composition caused by the industrial revolution, and right now you can pick up industrial and chemical pollutants that have blown their way up from European Russia across the Pole into the circulatory system above the High Canadian Arctic."

"How do you identify anything that specific?"

"What you're looking for are very fine sub-microscopic particles of soot which are quite diagnostic – that is, they clearly indicate certain substances which are not normally found in this area. Tie that in with what we know about the quirks of atmospheric circulation and you can tell where the particles come from."

"How do you obtain your sediments?"

"One of the great things about doing this work in the Canadian High Arctic is that you have ice sitting on the lakes for most of the year. So you can use it as a very convenient coring platform. What we do is to drill a hole in the ice and drop a coring device down into the lake bed a couple of metres or so. Up here, where the organic processes of nature take far longer than at warmer latitudes, it will have taken some 40,000 years for a mere two metres of lake sediment to be deposited."

We were talking at ten thirty at night. The sun, which had been hidden behind cloud for much of the day, was now shining brightly. Here in the High Arctic summer it would not go to bed at all that night. Nor, it transpired, would Roger. Outside, rotor blades were warming up. "That's my helicopter!" he exclaimed, and excused himself to race off to join his colleagues as they lifted off towards the frozen lake in search of new sediment cores and new insights into the distant past and possible future of our planet.

If, finally, you are after a really long perspective – millions or even billions of years – it is the geologists to whom you must turn. Ice, after all, normally comes and goes a great deal faster than rock. Even rocks have their tortoises and hares, however. The Himalayas, for example, are relatively recent products of the retreat of India away from the old supercontinent of Gondwana some 150 million years ago. The rocks from which they parted on the fringes of Antarctica directly to the south, however, are far older, more stable, changing more slowly.

In the Larsemann Hills on Prydz Bay, I met up with a research group of geologists from the University of Melbourne under Dr Chris Wilson interested in the early origins of mountain belts. 'Nomads' is what they call Chris and his colleagues back at the mother station, Davis, for they spend weeks wandering the hills, filling field notebooks with copious data, taking photographs and collecting rock samples – then return to what to them is the relative luxury of a field hut for a few days. It was in their hut one morning, with fierce katabatic winds raging outside and steaming mugs of tea before us, that I spoke to Chris and his Dutch colleague, Paul Dirks about their work. I asked Paul what had brought him to roam the exposed hills of Antarctica.

"In Europe, geologists talk about the Palaeozoic, which is about 580–250 million years ago. That's the kind of timescale you can study there. Down here in Antarctica we can look at rocks which go back to the Proterozoic which is anything from 600 million to 2.6 billion years old. And there are rocks near here in the Vestfold Hills and Rauer Islands which are Archean and could be as much as three billion years old!"

I asked about continental drift. For Chris and Paul, Gondwanaland is recent history, merely the latest example of the continents locking together. Asking a geologist interested in the Proterozoic about the supercontinent of Gondwana is like asking an historian about the day before yesterday. But I pressed on. Take the hills where we were meeting, for example; did these correspond geologically to those in India directly to our north? Is that how continental drift works?

"Parts of East Antarctica correlate with parts of southern Australia, Africa and India, certainly," said Paul. "When Gondwana broke up, bits and pieces came to be scattered all over the earth and formed new more or less stable continents. But other parts collided with one another and formed new mountain belts like the Himalayas. And while they were crashing into one another, one plate would 'subduct' beneath another. The part of Gondwana that was adjacent to this section of Antarctica became subducted under what is now Tibet – so that the only visible evidence left of that old continental crust is in this part of the world where we are sitting."

The break-up of Gondwana is still going on. The Himalayas, the Alps or the Andes and American Rockies, for example – mountain ranges caused by the movement of continental plates – are still rising by perhaps a few millimetres a year. But these mountain-building processes resulting from the subduction of one continental plate beneath another have only really been operative for the past 700 million years or so. And that is only about one-sixth of the age of the earth itself which is reckoned to be in the region of 4.2 billion years. So for about 3.5 billion years, rocks and mountains were formed in other ways that we know very little about because there are hardly any places on the entire surface of the earth where rocks of this age can be identified and studied. One of the very few such spots where you do have absolutely perfectly exposed outcrop is in the old Proterozoic terrains of Eastern Antarctica. Which is why the Nomads were there. What were they looking for?

"We're interested in the early origins of mountain belts," said Chris Wilson, "and in trying to decipher the various layers of mountain-building that have occurred in this region of the earth's crust. The rocks you see here were produced some twenty-five to thirty-five kilometres beneath the earth's surface, so we are also learning something about the processes by which they have been exhumed."

Our hut was in hills, but hardly a mountain range. Paul Dirks explained.

"A mountain belt formed about one billion years ago all along the edge of Antarctica here, several more or less parallel mountain ranges in fact. And it was roughly along this line, some 800 million years later, that the rupture began to form from which the supercontinent of Gondwana eventually began to break apart."

"So if we can learn how these mountains originated," added Chris, "and why they gave way when Gondwanaland drift began, we will be further along the road to understanding how the face of the earth looks the way it does today."

The winds began to die down as we drained the last mug of tea. The Nomads had to go back into the field and I was due to helicopter back to Davis. As I lifted off the ground I turned to take a last look at the two waving figures below and the rapidly diminishing outcrop of rock enveloped by Antarctic ice that they were studying: rocks dating back three billion years in some cases – nearly three-quarters of the presumed age of the planet itself.

Littering the approaches to the horseshoe harbour of Australia's Mawson Station during the brief summer thaw are any number of tiny rocky islets, as yet still not completely logged on hydrographic maps, each a potential threat to shipping. As you weave your way, dead slow, between these rocky outcrops and the treacherous shoals beneath the shallow surface, you will probably not spare a thought for the bewildering variety of curious Antarctic wildlife watching your manoeuvres from all sides. But these little islands, unwelcome as they may be to seamen, are oases for some of Antarctica's fauna – notably those most lovable of southern creatures, penguins.

We laugh at the penguin for its funny walk, flippers at its side like a gawky adolescent, the very model of dignified absurdity from the nonchalance of its upturned beak to its splayed, flat feet. Charlie Chaplin in a tuxedo. It is a bird yet it cannot fly, a kind of fish with wings. But watch a pair of skuas dive out of the air and peck at the eyes and neck of a penguin chick and then at its still writhing innards, or watch a leopard seal take an adult penguin and flay its skin off before consuming it, and you realise how vulnerable these creatures can be, at least on land. You cannot wander for long in the vicinity of an Antarctic penguin colony without encountering a corpse. Here, on the exposed rock surfaces at the bottom of the world, penguins accumulate in their millions: king, gentoo, rockhopper and macaroni penguins on the outer islands, chinstraps on the peninsula and, on the rocky outer edges of continental Antarctica itself, the Adélies. The real lords of Antarctica, however, are the emperors, often well over a metre in height and weighing as much as forty kilograms. The emperors break all the rules of lesser breeds, choosing to congregate on the Antarctic winter ice, nesting and breeding there, their eggs incubated by the male in a warm pouch on his foot while the female forages for food.

Most penguins, however, follow the more obvious polar pattern, seeking out a warmer, more sheltered habitat for nesting and breeding: in particular, the exposed rocks of the Southern Ocean. On one of the little islands just off Mawson Station, known (after another distinguished Australian scientist) as Béchervaise Island, is a small colony of some 5,000 Adélie penguins. Their sharp, black eyes, looking as though stitched on by a dollmaker, dart left and right as the birds waddle in from a good long swim, up towards a huddle of furry chicks waiting to be fed. They do not seem to notice, or at least to mind, that their progress up to the crèche has been constrained by wire netting, pushing them into a narrow pathway, over a little automated weighbridge. Many of the birds have identification tags implanted under their skin so that they can be individually logged as they go in and out of the colony, the time and body weight noted electronically.

Like seals, penguins may look faintly comic as they flip their way awkwardly over land, but as they slip into water, also like seals, they become instantly streamlined, graceful, powerful, purposeful. "Adélie adults can be away for as much as a week or ten days at a time," biologist Judy Clarke told me as we watched from afar. "They will swim, dive, rest – and

131

then be off again, always on the lookout for food. When they return to Béchervaise Island they can be a kilo heavier than when they left."

"Are you able to monitor where they go?" I asked.

"Up to a point. We've attached a satellite transmitter on to the backs of selected adults," she replied, showing me a large pad with antennae projecting out from it and looking rather like a giant upside-down cockroach. "These are stuck on to their backs and record details of their movements. They usually swim several hundreds of kilometres away from here to the continental shelf, seeking food. But precisely where they go we can't always determine."

"And what do they eat?"

"What they're looking for is krill, the pink, shrimp-like creatures that move around the Southern Ocean in swarms. Krill is good, high-energy food and good nutrition value too for the chicks. But when they can't find krill Adélies consume all sorts of fish.

"There's a strong sense of family loyalty among penguins, at least for each breeding season. The penguin will call when it comes into the colony – you can hear that 'caw! caw!' noise – and the chick will recognise the parent's voice and come running and call back."

Judy Clarke has to try to find out not only where the penguins have been to feed and how much weight they have put on – but what exactly they have brought back inside them. If you do not wish to kill them and cut them open, there is only one way of doing that. You look for birds recently out of the water, catch them, and place a tube gently down their throats. You then pump their stomachs full of warm water. When they are full and the water begins to dribble out of their mouths, you turn them upside down, massage their tongue and throat with your finger – and 'vomit' them. Much of the content of a penguin's stomach is undigested, so scientists can easily sieve it and make a careful lab analysis of the kind of fish or krill a particular bird has consumed and correlate this to some extent with time and place.

I looked around at the birds on Béchervaise Island and wondered which had been subjected to this humiliating treatment. A few yards away, an adult so tubby as to be clearly unmolested by Judy was being chased instead by a couple of downy chicks. Eventually, after a few tumbles, they all

132

Adélie penguins feeding their young by regurgitation.

stopped and the mother regurgitated some fish into the beak of one of the youngsters. "That's how the adults feed them," said Judy. "So regurgitation is not as unpleasant or unnatural an activity as it would be for you or me."

There is one other more obvious way of identifying, or at least guessing, what the penguins have been eating. I noticed that the rocky surfaces all around us were streaked with white. But I recalled that when I visited Bird Island just off South Georgia where there were perhaps 100,000 pairs of macaroni penguins, as well as smaller colonies of gentoos, the beaches were painted pink.

Judy explained. "At the moment, they're eating a lot of fish, so the guano they excrete is greyish white in colour. But in a few weeks' time the swarms of krill will materialise so the guano will become more pinkish for a while."

The changing pattern or colour of penguin guano correlates with the analysis of their food intake and this, in turn, begins to give scientists an important insight into the changing seasonal pattern of fish and krill in the oceans beyond.

All around the Antarctic, scientists are keen to know about the changing nature and content of the Southern Ocean. They are, indeed, enjoined by the Convention on the Conservation of Antarctic Marine Living Resources (CCAMLR) to do so. The devastation wrought by whaling and sealing in earlier times caused a massive disruption of Antarctic marine stocks with incalculable effects upon the entire oceanic food web evident to this day. But monitoring the contents of the oceans is more easily ordained than achieved. Ships keep logs of whale sightings and nations supposedly report their catches of fish and krill. But, even assuming this kind of evidence to be reliable, how do you know what is in the seas that ships do not visit?

This is where penguin studies are beginning to prove invaluable. In various spots around the perimeter of Antarctica other scientists, like Judy Clarke, are learning how to monitor the movement of penguins at sea and to analyse the contents of their stomachs. And as this information is gradually shared and correlated, a picture is beginning to build up of the fish and krill content of the Southern Ocean. This in turn helps CCAMLR to develop better informed policies as the nations of the world, always on the lookout for new marine resources, look hungrily towards the krill and fish stocks of Antarctica.

The best science often results from serendipity: the apparently chance findings of the open-minded practitioner whose hypotheses and experiments lead in directions he or she did not necessarily anticipate. The history of science is filled with legendary discoveries supposedly made in this way – from Archimedes' cry of "Eureka!" in his bath to the 'accidental' discovery by Fleming and his associates of penicillin. The truth is often less haphazard than the legend; serendipity is unlikely to work well for those who do not know what to look for. But, in polar science as elsewhere, carefully controlled experimental work can sometimes lead to unexpected results and even more surprising applications.

Take, for example, the work of Brian Barnes, a zoologist at the Institute of Arctic Biology at the University of Alaska, Fairbanks. He told me that he was studying the Arctic ground squirrel, a warm-blooded mammal of the Alaska North Slope which hibernates, it seems, a couple of feet below the ground, just above the permafrost, at a temperature below freezing point, living throughout the long Arctic winter off accumulated body fat.

"We're interested in finding out how animals survive in and adapt to extreme conditions," Brian told me. "Not just the severe cold of the Arctic winter, but also a long period with no light and, more critically, no food – then, suddenly, a summer with no darkness."

Brian led me downstairs, through a heavy door and into his cold and subterranean 'hibernaculum'. Lighting was low and temperatures lower.

"We try to mimic the conditions under which these Arctic ground squirrels overwinter on the North Slope," he explained. "We're at −5°C here but on the North Slope winter temperatures drop to −15 or −20°C so this is a kind of spring day for them!" He laughed, as he lit my way towards a series of drawers. It was like being in a mini-morgue. Brian pulled open one of the drawers and took out a plastic cage in which, curled up amidst a nest of wood shavings, was a fat, spiky-surfaced brown ball: a hibernating Arctic ground squirrel. He invited me to touch the animal.

"He's frozen," I said, pulling my fingers away.

"He's not frozen – but he should be. That's the trick."

"So what's he doing? Is he in a deep sleep?"

"No, he's not sleeping. I won't say he's awake though because his brain is so cold that I'm not sure it's functioning much. But he will respond to stimuli."

Brian touched the squirrel's prickly hair and the animal moved slightly.

"His heart rate has dropped from two or three hundred beats per minute down to only five or so. His breathing rate has dropped, too, from over a hundred respirations per minute down to a pattern of perhaps an hour or so with no breathing at all followed by about twenty-five quick breaths in a row and then another hour of no breathing and so on."

The squirrel was truly in a state of suspended animation – from which his internal body clock would cause him to emerge, Brian explained, in phase with external seasonal changes. "It's this kind of adaptation that seems to be required for small mammals if they are to endure the long, harsh Arctic winter."

"Why doesn't he migrate south?"

"His legs aren't long enough. The big animals – moose and caribou – they can migrate south. And really tiny mammals like lemmings can run around under the ground surface in the Arctic winter without using up too much energy or body fat. But this fellow here is betwixt and between, so he hibernates."

"Then he is only really functioning for a very brief period of each year?"

"That's right. The High Arctic summer only lasts three or four months and the ground squirrel has a lot to accomplish in that time."

"Like what?"

"Well, their reproduction period, for example, is very short, basically just the first weeks after they come out of hibernation. Then they regress back to an infantile state again, only to repeat the process the following year in a cycle of reversible puberty."

Not, on the face of it, a bit like human beings. Except that we, too, adapt our body rhythms to the external environment, adjusting when (for example) we travel east or west into a different time zone, or north or south into a different seasonality. Brian's squirrels, in their subterranean, artificial environment, were in fact hibernating right through the summer period, emerging into a warmer, lighter environment, which Brian can control, during the height of what in the external world would be the Arctic winter.

"It is this capacity to adapt to extreme and changing environmental conditions that interests us," Brian emphasised, "and from which there may be lessons for human beings."

We placed the squirrel back in his little drawer, put the lighting off again and made for the door. "He's really in a state that no human being can ever be in," I offered.

Brian replied enigmatically: "Well, that's yet to be established."

Brian Barnes' work has attracted a good deal of attention because of the potential application of this field of study to human organ transplant technology. Human blood functions normally at about 37°C. When blood cools, as it does in climbers who stay too long above 8,000 metres, for example, it gradually thickens and then, by the time it's dropped below zero, crystallisation sets in and the blood turns to ice — by which time, of course, the person is dead. There are some tiny animals in the Arctic (wood frogs, various insects) whose blood and tissues can freeze in the winter cold but who thaw in the spring and hop or crawl away apparently none the worse. But warm-blooded mammals like Arctic ground squirrels, whose body temperature drops to similarly low readings, cannot do this and seem instead to have a mystery mechanism that prevents their blood from freezing. It is this, crucially, that interests Brian Barnes and his colleagues.

It also interests the medical profession. At the moment it is possible to keep human sperm banks, blood plasma and some simple skin tissues for long periods of time by freezing them. But you cannot do this with an entire organ. So a human heart, liver or kidney is normally only available for transplant for perhaps two or three days at most.

"Suppose, however, that we could super-cool organs to those kinds of sub-zero temperatures without actually freezing them," said Brian, "they could then last perhaps a week or two and be available to a lot more potential recipients." Thus, the study of the hibernation patterns of Arctic ground squirrels could potentially save many human lives.

Another example of apparently esoteric Arctic science which could have surprising implications for human beings was revealed to me by Michael Castellini, a marine biologist also working out of Fairbanks. His work is on the breathing and sleeping habits of Arctic seals.

"The seal is a mammal. Like you and me he needs to breathe, yet he chooses to spend a lot of time under water where of course he has to hold his breath: diving, exercising, chasing fish – using up his oxygen supply rather than conserving it, it seems."

"How long does he hold his breath for?" I asked.

"A large, mature seal might stay under water for half an hour or more. The record is well over an hour. You or I can normally hold our breath for not much more than a minute or so at most."

There is another oddity too about seals that Mike Castellini pointed out to me: they also hold their breath for long periods while sleeping. Mike and his colleagues have been studying seal pups of about three to four months old and have found that these animals hold their breath while sleeping for perhaps thirteen or fourteen minutes at a time.

Then Mike told me that, in addition to breath hold and sleeping rhythms there was a third component to his study: heart rate. When these three factors are brought together some implications appear that could be of great significance for human beings. I asked him to explain.

"When sleeping seals hold their breath," he said, "one of the common things that happens is that the heart rate drops from the resting, awake value of let's say eighty or ninety beats a minute to a value of as low as fifty. That at least was the story we got from our three-to-four-month-old seal pups.

"Then, by accident really, we caught a pup of just three or four *weeks* old and instead of turning him back on the beach we thought we'd study him too. We knew the breath hold would be shorter. But what was a total surprise to us was that during breath hold this baby seal had a very poor ability to control the heart beat. We knew we were on to something really significant here which we didn't fully understand. So we went back into the field and focused on very young pups and confirmed that either the heart rate hardly dropped at all while they were breath-holding or, while the infant seal was holding its breath in sleep, the heart rate was extremely 'noisy', that is, very fast then slow, fast then slow and so on – quite irregular and poorly controlled."

"What happened as the pups got a bit older?"

"That's the interesting thing. We studied each seal pup again a couple of weeks later – and, lo and behold, the heart rate was both lower and more stable during the breath hold. A few weeks later still it was even lower and yet more stable, so that by the time the animal was around three or four months old – the age of the previous ones we'd studied – the heart rate was both extremely low and extremely stable."

Now most small children, too, hold their breath every now and then while sleeping; not as long as seals, but perhaps for ten or fifteen seconds at a time. And Mike Castellini believes that his researches on Arctic seal pups could help the medical profession to identify babies at risk from 'cot death' or Sudden Infant Death Syndrome (SIDS) who appear to have both a higher heart rate than normal infants and also very poor control of heart rate. Until now, he told me, most of the medical literature assessing infants at risk from SIDS has apparently concentrated on heart rate while the infant is breathing and not concentrated on these periods of breath hold. As a result of the work Mike and his colleagues are doing, the medical profession is starting to look also at how heart rate is controlled during these little periods of breath hold with a view to reducing the incidence of SIDS.

At the other end of the world, I met Peter Hirsch, Professor of Microbiology at the University of Kiel in Schleswig-Holstein.

138

Peter, a youthful and agile sixty-four-year-old (despite a hip replacement), was spending his fourth spell in Antarctica, this time working out of Australia's Davis Station in the Vestfold Hills. Like Brian Barnes, Peter told me he was interested in the way living organisms survive in extreme environments – in this case, the micro-organisms found in and on Antarctic rocks and lakes.

Germany has a long and distinguished record of polar scientific work. It was Alfred Wegener who first proposed the idea of continental drift, a theory that took forty years before finally achieving universal acceptance. Peter Hirsch, born and brought up near the Danish border where he still lives and works, did much of his early botanical work in northern Scandinavia. Nothing there was as cold, and as apparently arid and lifeless, as Antarctica. Yet here, on the Vestfold Hills, he told me he had found copious evidence of tiny biota able to survive the harsh Antarctic climate. In his careful and impeccable English, Peter talked to me about his work and some of its wider implications.

"We have been working, for instance, on the weathering processes of rocks," he said, "especially sandstone, and the ways in which the existence of micro-organisms help stimulate this weathering."

"Micro-organisms inside the rocks?"

"On the surface and inside them, yes. Now, the processes that we have managed to isolate in Antarctica can also be observed in old buildings in Europe. If you go to York or Chartres, they will tell you the building is deteriorating because of industrial grime and the chemical pollution in the air. But what we are now able to tell *them* is that there is also an internal, biological form of deterioration due to microbial breakdown caused by micro-organisms in the stonework, micro-organisms that would have been virtually impossible to isolate in an industrial city but whose behaviour we have been able to observe and codify down here in Antarctica."

And Peter Hirsch gave me another, even more unexpected example of the potential applicability of his research: its use to the detergent industry. I asked him to explain.

"The detergent industry is always on the lookout for protein-degrading enzymes. Normally, these enzymes work at high temperatures which is why, for a good wash, you have to do your laundry at 40°, 50° or 60°C if all the stains are to be removed properly. This of course uses up a great deal of heat, which is energy, and adds to the cost. But in Antarctica we are working on micro-organisms whose enzymes work at very low temperatures. And it may be that our research will reveal some that will enable you in the future to do a cheaper yet equally efficient cold laundry!"

Peter Hirsch and I shared a cabin on *Icebird* on the way back from Antarctica to Australia, and it was interesting to reflect, as our tiny cubicle strained day and night against the rough southern seas, that Peter's Antarctic rock samples, carefully secured down in the hold, might contain secrets enabling conservators to ease Notre Dame and the Parthenon into the twenty-first and twenty-second centuries – and enabling you and me to give our clothes a more cost-effective wash.

Much of the science carried out in the polar regions has repercussions far beyond its immediate results. Penguin studies, as we have seen, play a crucial role in helping to identify the changing nature of fish and krill stocks in an increasingly resource-hungry world. Upper atmosphere physicists working in the Arctic and Antarctic have learned much about magnetism and the solar system and have also been able to warn the world about the dangers of ozone depletion. A lengthy ice traverse can contribute vital data to the study of global climate. Scientists working out on the Arctic tundra among the bears and caribou have shown that methane, known to be a greenhouse gas, is released by melting permafrost and thus liable to feed back into a self-generating warming process melting the permafrost further.

As in all good scientific work, there is an element of hypothesis, of inspired guesswork, of certainty temporarily suspended as researchers grope their way more and more deeply into territory as yet not fully mapped. And this is palpably true, both metaphorically and literally, in the case of polar science. As our knowledge increases, it suggests yet further areas for research, new intellectual worlds to conquer, new frontiers to explore and chart. Yet, paradoxically perhaps, the further we penetrate the mysteries of polar science, the more the results appear to produce lessons of supreme importance and practical applicability to those of us living in the rest of the world.

140

CHAPTER SEVEN

Circumpolar Politics

On Tuesday 11 February 1992 at 3.30 p.m. an Australian helicopter left Davis Station on the Antarctic continent to drop a scientist at the nearby Rauer Islands. Suddenly, those in the helicopter were surprised to spot a ship no more than ten miles from land and they flew over to investigate. The vessel proved to be the *Nisshin Maru* from Tokyo and looked like a whale-processing ship. The Australians tried to contact the vessel by radio but received no response.

As they circled the *Nisshin Maru* they clearly saw whales being stripped and flensed. The decks were dripping with blood. A second Japanese ship nearby was chasing a small minke whale and the Australians watched as it fired its harpoon. At least one other Japanese ship was spotted in the vicinity. All the Japanese vessels could clearly see the helicopter observing (and filming) them and all would undoubtedly have been aware of their proximity to the Australian research station at Davis. None, however, announced their presence or made contact with the Australians in any way.

The incident was immediately reported to the Australian Antarctic Division and through them to the Australian government. The Melbourne *Age* reported the encounter prominently under a headline: "JAPAN IN POLAR WHALE KILL".

The whole affair caused great consternation and discussion at Davis that night and for many days thereafter. There was anger at what the Japanese had done; Australia has banned its own citizens from whaling and is, as we have seen, at the forefront of those nations wishing to conserve the pristine character of Antarctica. But there was frustration, too, since there was nothing Australia or anyone else could do about an event that caused revulsion and resentment.

The incident neatly encapsulates a number of different

The Nisshin Maru, *February 1992, a semi-flensed whale on deck.*

issues. The first is moral: many of the Australians were deeply upset as they watched the video taken from the helicopter of the David and Goliath chase and revolted by the barbarous fate of the whales once caught. Environmentalists emphasised the damage that whaling had done to the balance of marine life and were outraged that the Japanese were choosing to deplete the Southern Ocean's whaling stock still further. There were legal considerations too. The Japanese were permitted by the International Whaling Commission to catch up to 330 minke whales per annum for purposes of scientific research: observers were convinced they were taking more than that number and that the whales they slaughtered were destined not for scientific labs but for the restaurants of Tokyo. But could these suspicions be proved?

Finally, there was political resentment that the Japanese had been carrying out their grisly work so close to the coastline of Australian Antarctic Territory, within a few miles, indeed, of an Australian scientific base. "They were thumbing their noses at us," said one angered Australian that night, "and there's absolutely nothing we can do about it. We all know they're breaking the IWC rules. We only actually saw three dead whales on the deck. But there were probably 500 whales neatly flensed and cut up below deck. Yet short of monitoring their activities for many weeks how could we prove it?"

So the whalers are safe from sanctions as they go about their business. And the fact that the *Nisshin Maru* was less than a dozen miles off the coast of Australian Antarctic Territory? Australia's scope for complaint is considerably reduced by the Antarctic Treaty, to which both Japan and Australia subscribe, which not only puts all sovereignty claims into abeyance, but also effectively prevents any form of policing in the region. Thus, the Japanese whalers were breaking no treaty, no convention. They were technically within their rights to do what they did and neither tell the Australians nor ask their permission.

For many years the two polar regions were the backdrop for national posturing and rivalry. At the beginning of the century any event fractionally as provocative as the Japanese whaling affair could have caused a major diplomatic incident. Today, not only in Antarctica but increasingly in the Far North as well, national interests tend to be constrained by a shared desire for circumpolar co-operation. A glance at the map and a brief reading of polar history suggests why.

Mapmakers have a lot to answer for, particularly Mercator, whose two-dimensional, rectangular representations of the world create several kinds of distortion. In the first place, all lines of latitude are pictured equally: the equator, in reality some 40,000 kilometres around, is drawn the same length as 45°N or S (20,000 kilometres around) but also the Arctic and Antarctic which each converge on a single spot. Thus, areas in high latitudes are made to look wider than they are and places in lower latitudes narrower: Greenland on a Mercator projection of the world can be made to look vastly more extensive from east to west than India. The continent of Antarctica, though large, is made to spread right across the entire floor of the map.

This lateral distortion is compounded by the growing distances drawn between lines of latitude the further you go from the equator, so that Norway or Baffin Island, say, are made to appear far longer from south to north than, say, the similarly proportioned Malayan peninsula or island of Madagascar. The further away from the equator, in other words, the longer and wider all features are made to appear.

Other projections bring other distortions, and a wall map

elongating lower latitudes (an overlong Africa at the expense of a short, fat Greenland, as in the Peters projection for example) is no more accurate.

Many flat projections of the world place the equator lower than halfway down the picture. This is because most of the world's land area and the overwhelming majority of its population are in the northern hemisphere. The whole of India is north of the equator. Hobart, one of the southernmost cities of any consequence in the world, is on a comparable latitude to Detroit or Boston (Massachusetts). The Antarctic island of South Georgia is the same distance from the South Pole as Belfast or Newcastle-upon-Tyne from the North.

Pick up a globe, however, the only reasonably accurate way of representing our spherical planet, and at a glance it becomes obvious that, all flat projections notwithstanding, Greenland is in fact approximately two-thirds the size of India, that the continent of Antarctica is considerably larger than Australia, Brazil or Western Europe, that much of the southern hemisphere consists of ocean, and that Alaska lies at the hub of a wheel whose spokes reach out to Peking, Tokyo, Hawaii, Ottawa, Washington, London and Moscow.

Tilt the globe to put the South Pole in the middle and almost nothing is visible beyond the massive Antarctic continent and the vast ocean that surrounds it, though you may be able to glimpse the southern tip of Latin America, Africa, New Zealand and the island of Tasmania.

If you tip the globe the other way, however, and place the North Pole in the middle, a different perspective appears. Here, in complete contrast, is an ocean surrounded by land, a true 'mediterranean'. The land masses of the Far North ring the Arctic as though vying for space as lines of longitude converge: the Canadian archipelago stretching up in a lumpy triangle towards space also coveted by western Greenland; the Scandinavian 'dog' sticking its backside as far north as it can get; the great tier of Russia curving halfway around the entire polar rim, its baton finally handed over to Alaska (itself Russian until 1867) and then Canada once more.

Visit any of these Arctic countries and you will soon hear talk of the circumpolar North. Until recent times, say northerners, people tended to think of the Arctic as a series of separate extensions of its various national jurisdictions: the Canadian north (largely ruled from Ottawa), the Norwegian north (from Oslo), the Russian north (from Moscow) and so on. Today, they argue, when Greenland and Spitsbergen share computer terminals with Resolute (Canada), Barrow (Alaska) and Diksen (Siberia), this kind of north–south thinking is simply not good enough.

"When we meet our friends from Siberia or Greenland, we talk about common problems," says Gordon Wray, the *émigré* Scotsman who became Minister of Economic Development in the Government of Canada's Northwest Territories. "We discuss the latest techniques of building on permafrost or what kinds of winter fuel oils are most effective. And we talk about possible transportation links around the Arctic rim so that we can get to meet each other more easily. But every time I go to talk to people down in Ottawa or Toronto about our situation I find I have to explain everything from basics to them. The people in the south," he says, trying to hide his irritation, "simply don't understand."

Gordon Wray's frustration is reflected all around the Arctic. Everywhere, northerners complain that if you want to travel east or west around the Arctic you first have to go south. Decisions about the north, they will tell you, are made in the south for the convenience of southerners. In Tromsø, at the northernmost university in the world, professors of Arctic geology or glaciology wonder aloud, and with some resentment, why the Norwegian Polar Institute is in faraway Oslo. In Murmansk, it is the people in Moscow they complain about, in Greenland the people in Copenhagen, and in Fairbanks, Alaska, the folks down in Washington, DC.

"Sure we complain," said one Alaskan academic after moaning into his beer about the incompetence and ignorance of those in the south. "But you know the old saying: it's better to light a candle than to curse the darkness." And with that he launched into an upbeat list of some of the things polar people have been doing to help bring decision-making northwards.

There is, for example, the International Arctic Science Committee (IASC), set up in 1990, which provides a forum for scientists all around the Arctic rim to co-operate over research and share results. In Antarctica a similar body (SCAR – the Scientific Committee on Antarctic Research) has existed for many years. Native communities all around the Arctic are becoming increasingly active in the Inuit Circumpolar Conference (ICC), a body formed back in the 1970s but which only in the late 1980s began to enjoy full participation by representatives of native people from the largest of all Arctic countries, Russia. In Alaska, native peoples are once again able to link up with their distant cousins across the Bering Straits, while the latest chic tourist trip is to fly Alaska Airlines across the Straits and visit Provideniya and the former gulag town, Magadan, while Norwegian and Russian operators have set up shipping links between Kirkenes and Murmansk on the Barents Sea.

Circumpolar thinking is nothing new to the people of the Far North. Speak to a biologist like Frank Williamson of the University of Alaska, Fairbanks, a transported Californian who has lived in Alaska since before statehood in the 1950s, and he is quick to emphasise that many identical species are found right around the polar rim.

"More than any other place on earth," he told me, "the plant and animal communities of the high latitudes are remarkably similar. There are hosts of circumpolar species, and members of circumpolar groups that are closely related, solving their problems in very similar ways."

Nor is this all. "These things are also threatened in a circumpolar way, too, by movements in the atmosphere – for example by industrial contaminants drifting across the Arctic Ocean causing atmospheric haze and acid precipitation and therefore reduced biological productivity of lakes and streams. There's a lot of destructive material moving around the top of the world!"

Scientifically, circumpolar thinking has been a *sine qua non* for many years. Even during the Cold War, regional meteorological and climatic data were shared right around the north polar rim. Today, as Arctic scientists investigate the complex possible causes and effects of global warming, circumpolar co-operation has become utterly indispensable.

The circumpolar Arctic is in many ways the Last Frontier – one of the few areas on earth where much still remains economically undeveloped, where at least some of its resident populations are still able to pursue a lifestyle to some extent independent of industrialisation and other mainstream economic and social changes of the past 200 years. As we have seen, the issue of economic development is hotly debated right around the Arctic rim as people struggle to strike a balance between the various claims of native peoples wishing

146

to improve their material situation while attempting to retain a traditional culture, environmentalists concerned to prevent harmful or indiscriminate exploitation of the world's dwindling wilderness areas – and the governments and corporations from the south eager for a complex mixture of social, political and economic reasons to make the most of whatever sources of wealth and energy may remain untapped in their northern territories.

Yet while parts of the Arctic rim resemble the old Yukon still awaiting its Gold Rush, the circumpolar North is also in many ways a New Frontier, a region where the latest developments in hi-tech computer and satellite technology receive some of their most sophisticated applications, a veritable "window to the ultimate frontier of space", in the graphic words of Luis Proenza of the University of Alaska, Fairbanks. In such a world, it is inevitable that the petty localisms and nationalisms of the past should give way to broader regional perspectives.

If the Arctic is coming increasingly to be regarded as a unity, circumpolar thinking has a much longer lineage in Antarctica. From earliest times, navigators and mapmakers assumed, and then gradually confirmed, that beyond the southern seas there was a great cold continent of some kind: 'Terra Incognita', 'Terra Australis'. In the 1770s, Captain James Cook reported not only that the Southern Ocean, unlike any other, engirdled the entire world, but that further south at all points you would be likely to encounter an apparently impenetrable combination of snow, fog, ice and icebergs.

Cook never saw the continent of Antarctica, reaching only the walls of fog and pack-ice that tend to encircle it, and was never quite sure what lay beyond. But in the nineteenth century, various explorers, building on the legacy of Cook, pushed their vessels even further south, dodging in and out of the thinning summer pack and eventually reaching the sheer wall of ice that proclaims to every mariner: thus far and no further. There is still some dispute as to whose expedition was the first to reach or set foot on the continent of Antarctica. In 1820 the Russian explorer Bellingshausen sighted what he thought was an ice field "covered with small hillocks", while in the same season Edward Bransfield of the British Royal Navy reached islands that we now know to be part of the

147

Antarctic Peninsula. It is in any case a moot point whether, on reaching one of the Antarctic ice shelves that project out beyond the continent, you have in fact reached 'land'. No matter. By the end of the nineteenth century it was generally believed that there must be a great continent clamped to the bottom of the world with the South Pole in the middle.

What historians like to call the Heroic Age of polar exploration are the last years of the nineteenth century and the first two decades of the twentieth. This was the time of Scott and Shackleton, Nansen and Amundsen, Mawson, Peary and Stefansson. The North and South Poles were both discovered or conquered, and the Northwest and Northeast Passages both finally navigated. Epic tales were recorded of man's struggle against the elements. To this day the death of Scott or the survival of Mawson against unbelievable odds make riveting reading, while Shackleton's successful bid to save his comrades marooned on Elephant Island must rank among the most courageous rescue stories ever recorded. There was something heroic about these men, something larger than life in their vision, ambition and achievement. Only a giant among men could have conceived, as Nansen did, the bold idea of testing his theories about the Arctic Ocean currents by deliberately getting his purpose-built ship caught in the polar ice in order to drift with the current for the next few years. Only someone of almost superhuman will power (or arrogance, perhaps) could have stuck as single-mindedly as Peary to the goal of being the first to reach the North Pole.

There were other firsts to be achieved in later years: the first person to fly to or over each Pole, the first expedition to march to the North or South Poles and carry on walking, coming back the 'other' way, and so on. But in general, the 'Heroic' age gave way during the inter-war years to an era of mechanised exploration. One section of coastline was investigated and charted by the Norwegians, another by an American expedition, a third by Australians and New Zealanders. The British sent a team to learn more about 'Graham Land', the curious peninsula that juts out as though trying to meet the southern tip of Latin America. These exploratory expeditions were usually accompanied by a certain amount of flag-waving, flag-planting and flamboyant assertions of national sovereignty over a land area stretching nominally to the Pole itself. In this way, some of the contours of at least the outer rim of the great southern continent began to be known, like the edges of a great jigsaw puzzle, while the nations of the world claimed unto themselves increasingly fat slices of the still largely unexplored Antarctic pie.

There was no scramble for Antarctica quite like the crude imperialism to which much of Africa had earlier been subjected. Antarctica was clearly harder to reach and to penetrate, and its economic or military value more questionable. Yet the advent of World War II gave every region on the globe some potential strategic significance, including the Antarctic. The British worried that the Germans, perhaps with Argentine connivance, might be able to use the Antarctic Peninsula as a temporary submarine base from which to threaten Allied shipping lanes across the Atlantic. They therefore established Operation Tabarin which, working out of the Falkland Islands, kept watch on the south Atlantic. After the war the operation was renamed the Falkland Islands Dependencies Survey (FIDS, the predecessor of today's British Antarctic Survey) which, although initially motivated by strategic considerations, helped lead directly to what one might call the 'Scientific Era' of Antarctic investigation.

This was resoundingly launched by the International Geophysical Year of 1957–8. It was not the first such event. There had been a Polar Year in 1882–3 and another fifty years later in 1932–3. But the IGY was to be an altogether larger affair. For a start, even if its main thrust was directed towards the polar regions, it was planned to deal with the geophysics of the entire planet. It was to last a year and a half so as to encompass the full seasonal cycle of both hemispheres. And it was sponsored by the United Nations with the enthusiastic support of the two rival superpowers, the USA and USSR.

When the IGY was launched the Cold War was at its height. In 1956, the Soviet Union forcibly stamped out revolt against its hegemony in Hungary and Poland, while by the end of the decade any serious *détente* was indefinitely postponed as the Soviet leader, Nikita Khrushchev, stormed out of a Paris meeting with US President Eisenhower after confronting him with evidence of American aerial espionage. A decade that began with the Korean War ended with the nuclear arms race at its height, while the early sixties were to witness the erection of the Berlin Wall and a superpower confrontation over Cuba in 1962 that brought the world nearer than at any other time to nuclear war.

Yet not only was the IGY to prove a model of scientific and political co-operation. More, all agreed that the good work and goodwill evinced on all sides during the IGY should be retained and built upon. The result was one of the most imaginative and successful international accords of the century: the Antarctic Treaty, drawn up in 1959 and put into effect in June 1961. The Treaty happened because both the Americans and the Soviets, each anxious to place restrictions on the strategic ambitions of the other, wanted it to happen. As both powers groped towards an attempt to add some stability to a dangerous world, Antarctica seemed the perfect place to start. If the co-operation of the IGY could be extended indefinitely in Antarctica, there might even be lessons for the management of more obviously controversial areas of the world.

The Treaty defines Antarctica for practical purposes as all land south of 60°S and Article I insists that Antarctica "shall be used for peaceful purposes only" and prohibits "any measure of a military nature" such as the establishment of military bases, the carrying out of military manoeuvres or the testing of weapons. In particular the Treaty says that "any nuclear explosions in Antarctica and the disposal there of radioactive waste material shall be prohibited."

The Treaty enjoins its signatories (see Appendix) to maintain the scientific impetus achieved during the IGY and to exchange information about what they are doing in Antarctica and what scientific observations they come up with.

On the tricky question of political rights in Antarctica the wording is very careful. Nothing in the Treaty, says the text, "shall be interpreted as a renunciation by any Contracting Party of previously asserted rights of or claims to territorial sovereignty in Antarctica". Nor, however, can any acts or activities taking place while the Treaty is in force constitute a basis for "asserting, supporting or denying a claim to territorial sovereignty in Antarctica. No new claim, or enlargement of an existing claim," it concludes, "shall be asserted while the Treaty is in force."

All areas of Antarctica, finally, must be open to inspection at all times to representatives of other Treaty signatories.

The Treaty is remarkable not only in the history of Antarctica but also in diplomatic and political history. For a start, the

150

negotiating powers had to face the competing sovereignty claims of the various nations around the table. Australia claimed forty-two per cent of the entire Antarctic continent. Britain, Chile and Argentina made territorial claims that overlapped. The French insisted on their bit. So did the Norwegians and New Zealanders. One large section of the continent was (and still is) claimed by nobody. No Treaty could conceivably be signed until and unless these complex and emotive territorial issues were faced and somehow accommodated to everybody's satisfaction.

This was eventually achieved by the novel and face-saving device of holding in abeyance all claims for the duration of the Treaty. No signatory would either recognise or deny the territorial claims of any other (which is why the Japanese whaling ship operating a few miles off Australian Antarctic Territory in 1992 did not have to signal its presence). The two super-power signatories, the USA and USSR, pointedly made no claims to territorial sovereignty, but equally asserted that they and all Treaty signatories had right of access to any sector in the entire continent. The American base at the South Pole, encompassing as it does all lines of longitude, neatly encapsulated that claim, as did the Russian policy of spacing scientific stations at wide intervals around the continent.

In addition, the Antarctic Treaty represents the first and so far the only really successful attempt to declare a major region of the world free of any kind of military activity. The Cold War context in which the Treaty was originally drawn up and signed makes this particularly impressive, though it is easy to imagine the Soviet and American negotiators pressing for these provisions as a way of denying hypothetical advantages to the other side rather than out of any sense of virtuous self-denial. Whatever the motives, the demilitarisation of Antarctica was an important achievement, while the prohibition of nuclear explosions or of the disposal of nuclear waste was to prove something of a model for subsequent attempts to declare as nuclear-free zones such areas as Latin America, the South Pacific and the moon.

The prominence given in the Treaty to "freedom of scientific investigation" and the exchange among signatories of the results of their scientific work also represented a breakthrough at a period when the two superpowers were each treating scientists who shared nuclear secrets with the other side as spies and traitors.

The Antarctic Treaty has worn well. Its principal decision-making signatories, the 'Consultative Parties', have successfully fought off a recurrent challenge at the United Nations, led by Malaysia, to the effect that Antarctica should belong to the world, and be governed by the UN, not to a handful of self-appointed guardian nations. To these arguments, the Consultative Parties have riposted that, between them, Treaty signatories represent the great majority of the world's population (an argument enormously boosted when China joined their ranks in the mid-1980s) and indeed to the original twelve signatory powers have been added a further twenty-eight. In addition the Treaty has given rise to a number of bodies each with authority under the Treaty over some aspect of Antarctica, notably the Commission for the Conservation of Antarctic Marine Living Resources (CCAMLR). Environmental issues are increasingly at the forefront of attention and the 1991 Madrid Protocol not only proposed a ban on all mining in Antarctica but envisaged the establishment under the Protocol of a Committee for the Protection of the Antarctic Environment.

One of the articles in the Treaty declares that if any member wishes, thirty years after the Treaty comes into force, to review its workings, a meeting should be called to do so. That thirtieth anniversary came and went in 1991 with none of the members wishing to rock what was still evidently an astonishingly steady boat.

Australia's Davis Station, named after Captain John King Davis, lies on the coast of the exposed Vestfold Hills, some 8,000 kilometres south of India. It is a teeming little town of perhaps eighty people in summer and thirty in winter, mostly living and working in clean red, green and yellow buildings, many constructed in neo-Legoland modular, whose centre of gravity is a two-storey living-and-dining centre that would not disgrace a well-endowed provincial college. The copious club room contains a billiard-table, record player, bar and a series of windows with superb bay-and-iceberg vistas. Stroll down the wooden walkways and you come across older buildings, huts and shipping containers for the most part. These include the earliest sleeping quarters on base, the somewhat ramshackle but still cosy 'old donga line' – single rooms with a

Neo-Legoland modular at Australia's Davis Station.

curtain instead of a door and the bed seven feet off the ground to make living space beneath: primitive and only used nowadays for the summer overflow, but still regarded by old-timers with special affection.

There is biology at Davis, and 'Auroral and Space Physics', both with grand new buildings being completed when I was there by the ubiquitous representatives of the Australian Construction Service (ACS). The latest satellite technology permits Davis-based meteorologists to feed local met data into the international system. Fresh water supply can be a problem at a place like this, though ablution requirements are largely satisfied by plugging the station supply into the large self-enclosed pools caught in the bleak and arid hills nearby. If ever Australia decides to build a hard airstrip in Antarctica (as opposed to the ice runways which some countries use), it would probably be at Davis. There have in fact been a number of feasibility studies at various sites along the rocky roadway behind the station quaintly dubbed 'Airport Road'.

People at Davis like to call their station the Riviera of the South and it is remarkably warm and ice-free for Antarctica, partly because of the glacial drainage patterns off the ice plateau. Microbiologists at Davis find copious biota to study in the nearby lakes and there are a number of larger animals in

153

Apple and melon huts at Law Base.

the vicinity, most conspicuously a group of elephant seals, immense marine slugs that wallow on the beach, yawning, belching and snorting at each other. Dr Patrick Quilty, one of the top scientists at the Australian Antarctic Division, told me that it was just along from Davis a few years ago that he had come across the remains of what proved to be dolphin bones dating back about three million years – a discovery that threw into some confusion prevailing theories about the position and climate of the Antarctic continent at that period.

Dotted strategically on various offshore islands and in the Vestfold and Larsemann Hills over an area of several hundred square kilometres is a series of little satellite bases, well-provisioned overnight huts for the convenience of field parties studying the rocks or wildlife or whatever of the region. Law Base, for example, named after Phillip Law, the founding father of the Australian Antarctic Division, consists of a main hut with food and medical supplies, and little curved 'apple' or 'melon' sleeping huts pinned down to the rock against the katabatic winds that howl down every night and morning from the icecap. It may seem primitive if you are used to central heating, running water and flush toilets but provides an oasis of luxury to geologists in from a three-week camping trip. Set in the Larsemann Hills, a good forty-five-minute helicopter

154

ride from Davis, Law is the furthest of these satellite outposts. Indeed, its nearest neighbours are not Australians at all but Russians and Chinese, each a matter of a few kilometres away.

The Russians are among the original signatories of the Antarctic Treaty and they have bases deployed strategically in most sectors of Antarctica. If you were Australian and given to paranoia you might have wondered during the height of the Cold War, which was also the period when most of the initial Antarctic bases were first laid down, why the Russians seemed to be placing theirs at regular intervals around the Antarctic perimeter in apparent leap-frog formation with your own.

The station near Law Base to which I trekked with four Australian colleagues one blindingly beautiful Antarctic day is in fact a relatively recent one – or, to be precise, one of a pair of recent ones: Progress I and II. The Russians established themselves in the Larsemann Hills in the mid-1980s only to discover that the wind patterns and other local conditions made their new base almost unusable. So Progress II was set up a few kilometres away in a slightly more protected area. Morale was no higher than could have been expected as the Russians began to demolish their old camp and build up its replacement. 'Regress I and Regress II', they wryly dubbed the old and new stations. Shiploads of heavy supplies were unloaded in the magnificent bay at the foot of the hills and brought up to the new site by helicopter. A two-storey wood-frame office and accommodation building was commissioned from the Czechs.

When I visited Progress II in February 1992 that building was erected and nearly ready to receive its first occupants. "When will people move in?" I asked Sasha, the base doctor.

"Very soon."

It seemed wise not to press the question further. Sasha and his colleagues had been shipped out here in October 1991 as representatives of Mikhail Gorbachev's Soviet Union. They were due to be picked up in March 1992, the end of the southern summer, and to return to Boris Yeltsin's Russian republic. No, Sasha told me, they didn't have a Russian flag to fly – but there was certainly no evidence of the old hammer and sickle. What was in evidence was the stringent economic problems that had come to afflict Mother Russia. When the last supply ship had come in to Progress II a few weeks earlier it had brought a lot of letters but little food other than a few extra bags of potatoes. Our own small gifts were received with the gratitude of people under siege. The salaries being paid to Russians working in Antarctica were scarcely sufficient to sustain the families they had left back home – and out here they were in no position to bargain for more or look for alternative employment. Several I met hinted darkly that they were not even sure they would have jobs to go home to when they returned in March. Would anyone stay here after March? There would be no overwinterers, I was told; Progress II would close down for the winter.

As is the way on these occasions, my Australian friends and I were made enormously welcome during our visit to Progress II. No people on earth are more hospitable than Russians and, while we were keen not to consume any of their meagre provisions, we eagerly accepted mugs of steaming hot tea and the most overwhelming good cheer. One of the great achievements of the Antarctic Treaty is to develop among its signatories a tradition of mutual visits, and a genuine camaraderie exists between the various nationalities South of Sixty not quite paralleled anywhere else on earth. A few years ago the Russians went to extraordinary lengths to help fly out a couple of injured Australians based at Davis who had had an accident in the field. As there is no airstrip at Davis, the Australians helicoptered the two injured men over to the ice runway near Progress to which the Russians sent a plane from their larger base at Mirny. The two men were then flown via another Russian base to Maputo in Mozambique whence they were able to return to Australia for the hospital treatment they needed. Without the Russian help there is no way the injured men could have left Davis for Australia until the next supply ship visited. And all this was done by the Russians for no charge.

My Australian friends and I sat drinking our tea in Progress II in a little room adjoining the station's noisy generating plant. Sasha introduced us to his colleague Sergei, a rubicund young man who explained in fractured English that he was an electrical engineer. Ah, said Sasha, but what 'Seriozha' really likes to do is to make music – and with very little persuasion the young electrical engineer rummaged behind a pile of clothes, tools and discarded oil cans and emerged grinning with a balalaika. He played and sang a series of archetypal

156

Volodya and his tank.

Russian songs, alternately military and maudlin and sometimes both, while we listened, clapped in rhythm and marvelled at these warm-hearted men who managed to keep their spirits so high.

We were due to go on to the Chinese base, Zhong Shan, for dinner that night, a twenty-minute walk across hills and rocks, and were by now of course hopelessly behind schedule. No matter. Volodya would take us there in his tank. Volodya, an aeronautical engineer by vocation, is one of those plucky Russians who, by sheer force of personality can bluff his way in an audacious mixture of half-learned languages into or out of almost any situation he finds himself in. You may laugh at a squat military-style tank in Antarctica, but with Volodya at the controls this all-purpose vehicle proved capable of negotiating every kind of terrain Antarctica threw in its way as we rolled across from Russia to China.

The Chinese are relatively recent arrivals in Antarctica, having signed the Treaty only in 1983 and become one of the decision-making Consultative Parties two years later. They have two bases: Great Wall Station which huddles alongside those of many other nationalities on King George Island at the northernmost tip of the Antarctic Peninsula just across from Latin America; and Zhong Shan here in the far more secluded

Larsemann Hills where their only neighbours are the Russians and the Australians. They, too, revel in the opportunities for international camaraderie encouraged by the Antarctic Treaty. When *Icebird* arrived at Davis, their ship, the *Ji Di*, was anchored out in the harbour making a courtesy visit to the Australians before returning to the Chinese base down the coast.

As Volodya's tank pulled itself up the last of the stony hills towards Zhong Shan I saw a neat row of clean, squat buildings facing a courtyard flying the flags of Australia, the People's Republic of China – and the now defunct Soviet Union. I don't suppose the Chinese had an authentic Russian flag to fly any more than the Russians themselves did; but I suspect that even if they did they would not have displayed it.

We were ushered into what was clearly a more prosperous, or at least more self-confident, Antarctic station than the one we had just left, offered drinks and treated to one of those long, slow, toast-filled banquets diplomats write about in their memoirs. Plates appeared crammed with irresistible seafood delicacies – prawns, crabsticks and the like – and others (stringy jellyfish salad for example) that were easier to resist. Red and white wine was poured, though the alcoholic highlight was the Chinese vodka that was lavishly purveyed. Toasts and goodwill burgeoned as dishes of hot, fresh dumplings appeared. And all the while, the likeness of Sun Yat-sen, that most universally admired and safely uncontroversial of twentieth-century Chinese leaders, looked down benignly at us from his place of honour on the wall.

The Russian and Chinese bases, just that much further west than Davis, keep their clocks two hours behind the Australians. So, while my companions and I were reeling from a hard day's sociability, the Chinese were bright and fresh and keen to show us every nook and cranny of their station. Out we went into the late-night Antarctic twilight, shielding ourselves from the katabatics that were just beginning to howl across from the ice sheet above, to be shown the meteorological station, the science labs, the generator, the waste-water disposal plant and the rest – all evidently highly cost-effective and efficiently run. I cannot pretend to have taken in all the details or to be in a position to judge the quality of the science carried out at Zhong Shan. But I can report on a station that was clearly proud of its up-to-date equipment and whose denizens knew they basked in the confidence of the government back home who had sent them there.

Eventually we had to say our farewells and thankyous – and there parked on the Chinese forecourt was the indefatigable Volodya with his tank offering to drive us back over the Antarctic rocks and hills to Law Base. Over late-night drinks (or early-morning drinks if like us you were on Davis time) he and Sasha spoke of the Russia they had last seen many months back, their apprehensions, above all their love of Antarctica. "Where else in the world would a Russian tank drive British and Australian friends over to the Chinese for dinner?"

Next day we helicoptered over the ice back to Davis. Before we finally sailed away from the region, the captain of the Chinese ship, the *Ji Di*, heard from our voyage leader James Shevlin that *Icebird* had delivered thirty drums of fuel oil to Davis that the Australians had to helicopter down to Law Base. "I'll do it," he offered. "Just put them in our hold and we'll take the oil down there for you." Where else but in Antarctica . . .

Why are the various Treaty nations in Antarctica at all? "For science" is the conventional answer, one emblazoned on the publicity material most Antarctic nations produce and endorsed by the opening section of the Antarctic Treaty itself. Nor can there be any doubt of the importance of much of the science that has been and is being conducted there. Studies of stratospheric ozone, climate change, plate tectonics and continental drift, the oceanic food chain – these and many more are at the cutting edge of global concerns.

But hard-headed and hard-pressed governments do not pay big money to place people on the frozen continent purely for the sake of science. The cost of sending and supporting an Australian glaciologist overwintering in Antarctica and perhaps spending the summer months in a glacier field camp can approach A$100,000. The annual budget of Australia's Antarctic Division is in the region of A$60 million. So, is Australia there for the science?

"Not primarily," says one distinguished expert with remarkable candour. "We're there for political reasons. Antarctica is a vast continent not far from Australia. Sydney or Hobart are a lot nearer Antarctica than they are to Perth. Antarctica's our Near South, so we need to know what's going on there, to be present when decisions are made, to maintain a presence down there. Now if we're going to do that, what better way than maintaining a series of scientific bases? It's a cheap form of foreign and defence policy if you like, a way of keeping an eye on our back door. And science is the form our presence takes."

Much the same could be said of other nations, especially those in the southern hemisphere. Argentina, for example, has long regarded the Antarctic Peninsula as a continuation of its own essential geopolitical sphere of influence. At the Argentine base of Esperanza on King George Island at the tip of the Peninsula, entire families are in residence and pregnant women have been encouraged to have their babies in Argentine Antarctic Territory – a quaint way of asserting national sovereignty in the region.

Northern hemisphere nations, too, perceive Antarctica in partly political and strategic terms. The budget of the British Antarctic Survey was greatly increased in the wake of the Falklands War of 1982 – not surprising when it is recalled how BAS arose out of the Falkland Islands Dependencies Survey, itself the outcome of Operation Tabarin and before that of a history of Anglo–Argentine rivalries in the South Atlantic dating back to at least the beginning of the twentieth century. American interest in Antarctica, too, has always had an important political component. The largest expedition ever sent to the region (4,700 men, twelve ships and nine aircraft) was Operation Highjump of 1946–7 under the command of the veteran US polar explorer Admiral Richard Byrd. This was a massive assertion of American strategic interest in Antarctica, carefully staged in the opening years of the Cold War.

For all the laudable international goodwill and co-operation engendered by the IGY and the Antarctic Treaty, it is important to remember that Antarctica is not actually governed internationally. Territorial claims may be on hold but each nation runs its own scientific bases on a budget and according to rules agreed domestically. If you are accused of committing a crime in Antarctica you will be tried not by an international court but in the courts of the nation on whose base or in whose 'sovereign' territory the alleged crime occurred.

Some argue that claims of sovereignty should not be frozen but abolished and that Antarctica should be truly an international protectorate. Malaysia continues to lead a predominantly Third World campaign for Antarctica to be taken over by the United Nations. Greenpeace and other environmental groups have proposed that Antarctica be declared a World Park. Others have suggested it be regarded as a conservation zone protected by an agreement somewhat on the lines of the International Law of the Sea. There is much to be said for some of these truly international scenarios for Antarctica and their desire to remove entirely all national political interests from the continent. However, the evident success of the Antarctic Treaty and the fact that its Consultative Parties include all the big guns on the UN Security Council and between them represent so much of the world's population means that, for the foreseeable future at any rate, the Antarctic Treaty, with all its intrusive national politics, will continue to hold sway.

There is no Prudhoe Bay in Antarctica, and no Nikel or Zapolyarnye either. But there is abundant wildlife, a growing tourist trade – and on the continent itself there are likely to be huge mineral resources.

"Likely? There's no question of it!"

I was talking to geologist Chris Wilson of the University of Melbourne one day as we looked out over the Antarctic continent from the warmth and security of our tiny field hut in the Larsemann Hills. He reminded me that, since Antarctica had once formed the centre of the supercontinent Gondwanaland from which many of the world's south-facing continents had drifted away some 150 million years ago, clear geological links exist between its former component parts. Thus, the mineral composition of the Antarctic Peninsula is in many ways similar to that of the Andes that it faces across the Drake Passage.

"If you piece together the information we have about the geology of those regions that were once part of Gondwana land and tie it in with the evidence we are garnering here in Antarctica itself," said Chris, "it is pretty clear that the potential mineral wealth of Antarctica is enormous. East Antarctica, for example, where we are talking at the moment, is part of the old Proterozoic continental shield area. Seventy or eighty per cent of all the mineral wealth in the world is provided at present by Proterozoic shield areas like this – Australia, Canada, Brazil, Russia, southern Africa – where there are rocks very similar to what we find here. So

161

Antarctica is without doubt full of potential mineral wealth."

"Of what kinds?"

"Lead, zinc, copper, silver, gold, uranium perhaps. Iron ore, coal deposits probably. A large variety. And in addition to all that we have continental shelf areas, like Prydz Bay here, where there are good prospects for gas and oil."

In earlier times, before the continent itself became accessible, the wealth people sought in Antarctica was at sea. Captain Cook's reports in the 1770s that he had seen fur seals when he visited the sub-Antarctic seas and islands gave rise early in the following century to armadas of sealing vessels around the Southern Ocean. The subsequent massacre, and some of the fortunes amassed, were immense; and the impact not only upon seal populations but on the entire food chain is still with us today. Whaling in the southern seas was to produce even larger fleets and fortunes, while in recent times heavy overfishing has added another chapter to the melancholy saga of man's indiscriminate plunder of the Antarctic Ocean.

In 1980, the Consultative Parties to the Antarctic Treaty signed a Convention on the Conservation of Antarctic Marine Living Resources (CCAMLR). This defined Antarctic waters as all that lay south of the Antarctic Convergence, that uneven belt around the Southern Ocean where warm currents from the Atlantic, Pacific and Indian Oceans encounter the cold currents of Antarctica. CCAMLR attempted to constrain all signatories to limit their harvesting of the southern seas to levels that would not damage the Antarctic marine ecosystem as a whole. 'Rational use' of these seas was permitted. But not to the point where stock might not recover, and not to the detriment of other marine life. CCAMLR (in conjunction with the International Whaling Commission) has been an important influence in helping to protect depleted fish and krill stocks, though no convention of this kind can be fully enforced. What could the other signatories do when the Russians and their then-allies in Eastern Europe, followed by the Japanese who were primarily interested in krill, systematically plundered the southern seas throughout much of the 1980s?

The problem of how best to maintain Antarctic krill, fish and whale stocks at stable levels is largely a question of sensible long-term environmental management: 'rational use' so that there will be more later. CCAMLR is not a perfect instrument, and by permitting some harvesting it has arguably left the door open to too much. What is rational to one country may be thought excessive by another, particularly since accurate numbers of oceanic stock are hard to establish. CCAMLR can neither police adequately nor adjudicate, and some experts continue to worry about the depletion of stocks and the deleterious impact this is having on the entire oceanic food chain.

It was in order to pre-empt precisely this kind of problem at an early stage that during the 1980s the Consultative Parties decided to try and hammer out a policy on the exploitation of Antarctic mineral resources. Here was an explosive issue, one potentially capable of dividing the Treaty signatories more than any other. They figured that, at the moment, no available technology permits comprehensive examination or extraction of rock strata buried beneath two or three kilometres of solid ice. Nor are the costs of establishing and supplying mining or drilling operations in Antarctica over an iceberg-filled continental shelf remotely feasible at present. Surely, they felt, it would be better to work out an agreed approach now, when much of Antarctica's presumed mineral wealth was still largely unreachable, than to wait until new technologies of extraction and transportation introduced a glint of greed into the discussions.

So a series of complex negotiations took place and, after several years of hard-fought and sometimes acrimonious debate, a Convention on the Regulation of Antarctic Mineral Resource Activities (CRAMRA), which placed careful controls on mineral exploitation in Antarctica, was adopted in Wellington in 1988 and awaited signature by the governments concerned.

The following year, Australia, rapidly followed by France, changed its position in the most dramatic way possible, Prime Minister Hawke not only announcing that his government would refuse to sign the Convention but insisting instead on a new agreement that would cover environmental matters far more broadly and, among other things, ban all mining in Antarctica completely. This bold turnaround surprised many observers and was greeted with a combination of delight and incredulity by environmental groups. Cynics could not help wondering why people like Bob Hawke and François Mitterrand had suddenly become so 'Green'; could the U-turn have

Mawson Station dogs which must leave Antarctica by 1994.

anything to do with their flagging political fortunes at home?

A great deal of horse-trading followed* and in 1991 a Protocol on Environmental Protection was adopted in Madrid. Article Seven proclaims baldly and unequivocally: "Any activity relating to mineral resources, other than scientific research, shall be prohibited."

It was in the wake of the Madrid Protocol that I visited some of the Australian Antarctic stations in 1992. Never can environmental considerations in Antarctica have been so much to the forefront. The Australian Antarctic Division had recently appointed an Environmental Officer who was on the voyage with us with a brief to check on the environmental impact and practices of the various stations we visited. We also had as a guest on board a representative of the environmental coalition ASOC (Antarctic and Southern Ocean Coalition) who had previously visited a number of Antarctic stations with Greenpeace. Discussion on ship and shore regularly returned to environmental issues. How were waste

*And dog-trading. The Madrid Protocol included the statement that "Dogs shall not be introduced onto (Antarctic) land or ice shelves and dogs currently in those areas shall be removed by April 1, 1994." This caused much heartache at Australia's Mawson Station, one of the last in Antarctica to retain huskies.

products disposed of? What was the environmental impact of tourism in Antarctica? What kinds of Antarctic rock or moss samples could scientists legitimately take away from Antarctica? What were the least disruptive ways of studying Antarctic wildlife? What alien biota had the presence of humans brought to the world's last unspoiled continent? No issue was too small to warrant concerned discussion.

An excess of zeal? Possibly, though it has to be remembered that the environmental record of the Treaty powers in Antarctica has in the past left much to be desired. The huge American base at McMurdo, for example, was notorious for many years for the amount of junk lying around and for the obviously major and possibly irreversible impact it had upon the local environment. In the cold, dry atmosphere of Antarctica, even organic waste takes far longer to degrade than in damper, more temperate climates, and until very recently many nations were littering Antarctica with unsightly forms of mineral hardware, often harmful to local wildlife, that would probably remain for ever.

In the wake of the Wellington débâcle and Madrid Protocol, Australian behaviour in Antarctica was very much under the international microscope. Regarded by countries such as the United States and the United Kingdom as the nation that had upset the delicately balanced Wellington apple-cart, Australia had to be sure her own environmental record was beyond reproach. This meant of course that ships and stations had to be kept clean and that all rubbish generated in Antarctica was to be returned to Australia; also, that environmental impact assessments should be drawn up for stations and field camps and indeed all new activities.

In addition, the new environmentalism gave rise to a great deal of discussion about another economic issue that we have already encountered in the Arctic: the potential impact in Antarctica of increased tourism. Tourism in Antarctica is at the moment a tiny business: a matter of perhaps five or six thousand visitors per annum. Almost all go by ship, the great majority of them on tourist cruises from the tip of South America to the Antarctic Peninsula, though some also visit the sub-Antarctic islands of Australia and New Zealand.

The numbers are currently so small and the cost so high that, here as in the Arctic, there is little danger of hordes descending. Tourists, however, can make a disproportionate impact upon Antarctica. For a start, they are not spread out evenly over the year but tend to visit during a concentrated summer period of six or seven weeks. And of course many of them want to go to precisely the same areas as the scientists. Most of the land mass of Antarctica is inhospitable, buried beneath its vast icecap. This is not of primary interest to most of the tourists or most of the scientists. Both are more attracted to the peripheries of the continent, the more accessible edges of the icecap, the exposed rocks and islands that provide the habitat for the seals and penguins and albatross (and the areas most associated with the comings and goings of the great Antarctic explorers). These regions represent a tiny fraction of Antarctica as a whole but it is here that outside interests converge and potentially conflict.

One of the qualities that attracts scientists to Antarctica is that it is a vast pollution-free natural laboratory. Dr David Wynn-Williams, a leading British microbiologist whom I met at the British base on Signy Island in Antarctica, told me, "I can climb up the hill behind here each morning and study micro-organisms in an environment absolutely free of pesticides and fertilisers or the subtler man-made additives to the atmosphere back home – lead deposits and the like." This absence of local pollutants gives his research an international applicability it might not otherwise have.

What does he think of tourists? "I welcome their enthusiasm," he acknowledges, "but at the same time I recognise them as a potential threat to my work. In a way we are all visitors. Anyone coming down here – including scientists – is bound to have a destructive effect on what is an extremely fragile environment. A few thousand extra boot prints can threaten communities of microbes, mosses and lichens that take centuries to develop and support very complex but vulnerable ecosystems. The very process of taking a shipload of inadequately briefed tourists to see these mosses and lichens could completely destroy them. It's bad enough having thousands of fur seals rolling around the island!" he says – though quickly adds that they at least are indigenous.

What is the answer? Should the scientists have Antarctica to themselves? That hardly seems fair. Should the growth in tourism that everyone anticipates proceed uncontrolled? That is no answer either. There is clearly big money to be made from Antarctic tourism, at least potentially, and there has been talk of building hard airstrips and a hotel or two adjacent to some of Antarctica's more spectacular settings. But the environmental impact of this kind of undertaking would be unacceptable to the Treaty signatories at present.

One possible solution that has been proposed is to designate certain 'Antarctic Protected Areas' (APAs, on the analogy of the existing Special Sites of Scientific Interest, or SSSIs). These might be near but not at scientific stations, well-documented places, perhaps of historic interest, preferably full of typically Antarctic flora and wildlife which enthusiastic scientists from nearby stations could point out – from carefully designated spots – while having minimal impact upon the historic sites or the flora and fauna themselves.

The politics of Antarctica represent a unique experiment in non-sovereign government, a genuine accommodation between sovereign powers to remove at least one of the world's great continents from the worst ravages of national political rivalry. In practice, as we have seen, national politics play a part here as elsewhere; it is just that the nations concerned find it by and large to be in their best interests to continue to play by the supranational rules they have invented for themselves. In the Arctic things are in many ways exactly the opposite. There is no supranational Treaty here and we are back to 'politics as usual' – yet in the Arctic, too, we are witnessing the emergence of new, co-operative regional thinking. Let us start at one of the more remote land borders in Europe, that between Norway and Russia. Until recently this was one of the most sensitive land borders in the world. Here, far above the Arctic Circle, as nowhere else except beyond the eastern confines of Turkey, the forces of NATO and the Warsaw Pact faced each other directly across a shared frontier. As the Cold Warriors of East and West contemplated the unthinkable, this was one of the points on the map to which their attention inevitably turned.

Nor was Cold War tension in this region all in the mind. On both sides of the Pasvik River, substantial forces were assembled. They still are. In eastern Finnmark, you are periodically likely to come across areas where the hills bristle with military installations. And just in case you have not noticed there are large roadside billboards that, somewhat

A former Cold War frontier: the Pasvik river dividing Norway from Russia.

incongruously, first draw your attention to the fact and then tell you not to stop and look. On the Russian side evidence of military might is even more conspicuous. Indeed, the Kola peninsula, the Russian 'tail' to the Scandinavian 'dog', is one of the most densely militarised regions in the world. But this did not begin with the Cold War, nor is it likely to end just because the Cold War is no more.

Russia has for centuries been a land power in search of a sea outlet. In both Tsarist and Soviet times, Russian leaders made efforts to secure access to the Mediterranean to the south (by way of the Black Sea), the Atlantic to the west (via the Baltic) and the Pacific to the east. One consequence was that Russia found herself periodically thwarted by, and occasionally at war with, more nautically favoured neighbours. The Crimean War in the 1850s, for example, was in part a British attempt to restrict Russian access to the Mediterranean and the Russo–Japanese War of 1904–5 about keeping Russia out of the Pacific.

The one direction in which the Russians have undisputed access to the sea is to the north where they possess a vast swathe of coastline that curves almost halfway around the entire Arctic rim. Into the Arctic Ocean flow the great Siberian rivers – the Ob', the Yenisey and the Lena, three of the longest in the world: waterways that provide passageway for goods, people and services deep into the Russian heartland. For centuries, Russian and other sailors tried to press a passage right across the Arctic coastline from the relatively warm waters of the Barents Sea in the west through the ice towards the Pacific. This fabled Northeast Passage lured mariners from Willoughby and Chancellor, Barents, Hudson and Bering through to Amundsen and Stefansson in the early twentieth century. Some legs of the journey proved relatively easily navigable, at least during the summer months, and parts of northern Siberia were thus opened up to development – a process pursued with notorious vigour in Stalin's time.

Stalin actively encouraged northern development. Nickel, cobalt, tin, salt, gold and diamonds, apatite, lead and zinc, coal, gas and oil: all were known, or believed, to lie in great quantities precisely where the Soviet government felt most secure from foreign interference, near and around the Arctic coastline, especially northwest Siberia. Thus, for both political and economic reasons, Stalin looked north.

A vigorous development policy was instituted, complete with crash programmes to educate local natives in the benefits of communism and of dropping their own language in favour of Russian. Heavy machinery was shipped up the great Siberian riverways or across from Murmansk or Arkhangel'sk, and then dragged, flown or railroaded up towards the Yamal or Taymyr peninsulas (or even across the Verkhoyanskiy mountains) to the new mines or drilling sites. Slave labour was recruited from those deemed politically undesirable elsewhere, local minorities 'Russified' as a matter of urgency – and heavy industry promoted on a gigantic scale entailing a degree of planned human agony and degradation probably unmatched in history except perhaps in Hitler's Germany.

Topping all these policies was the necessity of keeping supply routes open. Ice-breaking capability was strengthened, and in 1932, for the first time, a ship, the *Sibiryakov*, managed to traverse the entire Northeast Passage, from the port of Murmansk in the west to the Bering Straits opposite Alaska in the east, in a single season: the culmination of a centuries-old dream, and the start of a new era in northern geopolitics as Soviet thinking attached ever-increasing importance to the Arctic littoral.

If anyone had any doubts about the supreme strategic

169

importance to Russia of its Arctic approaches, these would have been firmly laid to rest during World War II. In August 1941, Hitler turned against his erstwhile ally Stalin and sent invading troops deep inside Soviet territory. Russian morale was profoundly dented and at first it seemed that the great Soviet empire would totter just as so many of the nations of Western Europe had already done. But heroic resistance during the winter of 1941–2 kept the Germans at bay and aroused great admiration in Britain, the one European nation still effectively at war with Germany. How could the British (and Americans, who entered the War in December 1941) give practical help? One way was through naval convoys that would run the gauntlet through Nazi-controlled waters off the long coast of Norway, around the Norwegian North Cape, and thence down to the Russian Arctic port of Murmansk. It was risky, lives and *matériel* were lost – but it worked and was hugely appreciated in the desperately beleaguered Soviet Union.

Today, the harbour of Murmansk is dominated by a vast war memorial (to 'the Battle of the Soviet Arctic'): a giant helmeted Soviet soldier, erected in 1974, guarding the entrance to the Russian Arctic. At his feet is a flame to the unknown soldier. Russian school and tourist groups visit the monument to pay their respects and learn of an important chapter in the history of their nation. When I visited Murmansk, friends took me to a cemetery containing the impeccably maintained graves of British sailors killed during wartime convoys.

During the Cold War era, Murmansk took on even greater significance as the 'Gateway to the Arctic'. Much of the Soviet Union's western flank was relatively secure thanks to the imposition of Soviet military and political priorities upon all the nations of the Warsaw Pact. These Soviet satellite states acted as a buffer between the USSR and its Western adversaries in NATO. But no such cushion existed further north in the Kola peninsula. Here on the Norwegian–Russian border NATO stood at the very gates of the Soviet Union itself. From the Russian perspective this clearly demanded the highest degree of military preparedness in the region.

In addition to looking northwestwards with alarm the Soviets also looked due north across the Arctic Ocean and northeast across the Bering Straits where, again, what they saw was NATO: a tier of potent weaponry facing them across the other half of the Arctic rim in a mirror image of their own highly militarised northern coastline, from Alaska just across the straits, right around the vast Canadian archipelago, and the US bases in Greenland. If you look at the globe with the North Pole in the middle, the Arctic Ocean emerges as one of the most obviously crucial theatres of Cold War confrontation in the world.

Add to the geopolitics of the Arctic the rapid technological advances of the era and it becomes even more clear why the Arctic rim and its gateway port of Murmansk continued to be of such crucial importance to the Russians. If NATO were to attack from the west, much of their impetus would presumably have been neutralised by the presence of Russia's satellite states. But from Norway or Alaska the enemy was on Russia's doorstep while the entire northern rim was vulnerable to missile attack from across the Arctic Ocean. In the age of thermonuclear weaponry, the Arctic Ocean was a pond ringed by mutual hostility and the 'soft underbelly' of the Soviet Union was its north coast, especially its northeast and northwest regions lying so close to enemy territory.

Nuclear technology altered the Russian Arctic in another way too. During the 1950s and 1960s, ice-breakers were built of increasing strength and thickness. But the Northern Sea Route, containing as it often did even in the summer season hundreds of miles of ice three or four metres thick, remained an exceptionally difficult passage to navigate. Ships under steam could simply not generate the horsepower required to press their way through ice of this thickness. The ability to cut sea-lanes through this route each summer was a major Soviet priority. Here, too, nuclear technology was harnessed – and with spectacular success. The first of the giant Soviet nuclear ice-breakers, the *Lenin*, was commissioned as long ago as 1959. By the 1970s, the Soviets were committed to building up an entire fleet of nuclear ice-breakers, including the *Arktika* (1975) and *Sibir* (1977) both of which displayed their ability not only to navigate the entire Northern Sea Route but also to cut their way through multi-year ice to and beyond the North Pole itself. Other ice-breakers were commissioned by the Soviet Union from shipyards in Finland.

The home port for this fleet of nuclear ice-breakers was and is Murmansk, the largest city and the greatest port above the Arctic Circle. Here the Murmansk Shipping Company controls the largest fleet of ice-breakers in the world – and thereby access to and through half of the Arctic Ocean.

Murmansk was the home port, too, of the Soviet nuclear submarine fleet. Well over half of all nuclear ballistic-missile Soviet submarines were based here. In addition to the strategic significance of the Arctic in an era of superpower stand-off, nuclear-powered (and armed) submarines had a particular advantage in these regions: they could sail indefinitely and virtually undetected by enemy radar beneath the polar ice. The Americans pioneered the techniques and trumpeted the fact when the nuclear submarine *Nautilus* sailed beneath the ice to the North Pole in August 1958. Both superpowers must be presumed to have had armed submarines patrolling Arctic waters during the 1960s, 1970s and 1980s, their nuclear fuel enabling them to generate their own power almost indefinitely, their whereabouts remaining largely unknown to their adversaries.

Thus, by the mid-eighties, the Russians attached more importance than ever before to their vast Arctic region, considering it a major economic and strategic resource and defending it with massive armed forces on both land and sea. The whole region – including the sea and land approaches to Murmansk and the entire Northeast Passage beyond – was effectively off limits to all but a tiny number of authorised Soviet personnel. No foreign ships, even from fraternal communist nations, were permitted through the Northern Sea Route. Visitors to Murmansk normally had to fly in from somewhere like Moscow.

Then, on 1 October 1987, Mikhail Gorbachev, at the height of his influence, came to Murmansk to present the Order of Lenin and the Gold Star Medal to the city. The speech he made at the ceremony proved to be one of the most remarkable in the annals of Arctic history. "Let the North Pole," he said, "be a pole of peace." And he went on to list some specific and quite unprecedented proposals. First he suggested that northern Europe become a nuclear-free zone with the Soviet Union as guarantor, and went on to talk of ways NATO and the Warsaw Pact could de-escalate military tensions in the Arctic region. He turned to the immense energy resources of the Far North and proposed new forms of East–West co-operation in their extraction – specifically, an invitation to Canadian and Norwegian firms to join forces with Russian companies to

172

consider ways of developing oil and gas reserves in the Soviet Arctic. Gorbachev spoke, too, of greater scientific co-operation around the Arctic rim and of new opportunities for northern indigenous peoples to extend and share their ethnic and cultural aspirations. He spoke of the Arctic environment and the urgent need for an international, co-operative plan to protect a region in rapid deterioration because of the unthinking depredations of the recent past.

Finally, Gorbachev spoke of the Northern Sea Route. "The shortest route from Europe to the Far East and the Pacific Ocean passes through the Arctic," he said, and went on to propose "opening the Northern Sea Route to foreign ships, with ourselves providing the services of ice-breakers."

This was a quite astonishing speech in the breadth of its vision and its break with traditional Soviet policy. His reference in particular to the Northern Sea Route held out the prospect of utterly transforming world cargo routes. The distance from Stockholm, say, or Hamburg to Yokohama or Osaka via the Suez Canal is nearly double that via the Northern Sea Route – some 11,000 nautical miles as opposed to just over 6,000. Add to this the chronic political instability of the Middle East region and it is clear that Gorbachev was suggesting something that could be immensely tempting to the West – the possible fulfilment of a dream that dated back among Western European mariners some 400 years or more.

"The main thing," Gorbachev said by way of conclusion, "is to conduct affairs so that the climate here is determined by the warm Gulf Stream and not by the polar chill of accumulated suspicions and prejudices."

I was in Murmansk in August 1991, a couple of weeks before the anti-Gorbachev coup, and asked people what they thought about his famous speech of four years earlier.

"It sounded good. But like everything else he did it was aimed at the interests of audiences abroad and did nothing for people here in his own country."

I had to demur (doubtless thereby reinforcing their views). After all, I had arrived in Murmansk under circumstances that would have been utterly unthinkable before the change of policy. We had sailed from Kirkenes in Norway down the coast of the Kola peninsula, right through the Russian fleet, past the military city of Severomorsk, weaving our way between hosts of Soviet warships and submarines and down

173

Russian warship alongside Severomorsk on the Kola peninsula.

under the nose of Russian radar installations that lined the whole of the latter part of the route. One day during my stay in Russian Kola I drove southeast through the very heart of the peninsula, past any number of military camps. And when I returned to Norway a few days later I took a train. For nine hours the train had chugged its way through the Arctic boreal forest and tundra, halting every now and then at tiny villages whose hinterland visibly contained a series of huge armed camps. We had soldiers boarding or leaving the train whenever and wherever it stopped.

None of these journeys – by boat, car or train – would have been permissible during the period of the Cold War. All had been made possible by policies initiated by Gorbachev's Murmansk speech. And all were examples of *glasnost* in action. My Russian friends were perhaps right. The queues for food were dreadful, and there was much evidence of corruption and venality among those who held the levers of power. But the nation's links with the outside world were vastly improved, as my brief series of forays clearly illustrated.

"Of course they want Westerners like you to visit," I was told by a political journalist I met in Murmansk. "Because you bring hard currency!"

"But why let me sail right through the middle of your

174

nuclear navy?"

"I'm not sure the military are happy about that," came the reply. "But today, the need for hard currency is greater than that for secret defence forces. Also, it's a way they can show that it's the political people not the military who make the decisions."

It would be hard to exaggerate the political changes that have occurred right around the Arctic in consequence of the epoch-making developments in Russia. The entire rim is now abuzz with circumpolar co-operation, something never really possible as long as the largest of all Arctic countries remained secretive, suspicious and aloof. In 1989, the Arctic Games, held in Yellowknife, included Soviet athletes for the first time. The Inuit Circumpolar Conference now regularly includes representatives of the indigenous peoples of the Russian Arctic. All the governments of the Arctic rim, as a result of a meeting in the Finnish city of Rovaniemi, have agreed an 'Arctic Environmental Protection Strategy' and set up a task force to monitor the shared Arctic environment and to make practical recommendations for international action. Circumpolarity is evident at a more local level too. At the University of Alaska, Fairbanks, I ran into a professor of cultural anthropology on loan from Moscow who was making a comparative study of the indigenous Arctic peoples of Russia and America, and in Iqaluit in Arctic Canada a couple of visiting librarians from the city shortly to be renamed St Petersburg. The Norwegian town of Kirkenes was awash with visiting Russians when I was there, and the climax of a three-day summer festival was a football match between the border guards from the two countries who for so many years had normally spent their time staring suspiciously at each other across the Great Divide between East and West.

But perhaps the most interesting political development in the Arctic arises out of initiatives taken not so much by the various national governments as by the peoples of the region. For many years, as we have seen, indigenous peoples and their cultures were kept under strict controls. Native languages, religions and even traditional styles of music and dress were at best merely tolerated and often outlawed. As for the land on which native peoples had lived, travelled and hunted for many centuries, this was effectively annexed by those representing southern governments, often with not even the pretence of a treaty of agreement. Today, much of this is changing, and at a bewildering pace.

"The land belongs to the people!"

Lenin in 1917? No; a Canadian Inuk talking to me in 1991.

Who owns the land you live on, work on, walk on, ride on? And all that is above it and below it? Probably lots of different authorities and individuals. You may own the land on which your house is built, while the roads outside belong to the local department of transportation and through them various layers and levels of local and national government. Or perhaps you live and work in a building erected on rented land – rented from the State, the Church or some other vast and ancient corporate or individual landowner.

In many parts of the world, who actually owns the land is largely uncontroversial. Most people in Oslo or Ottawa, Madrid or Moscow accept that much of the land where they live is in the hands of giant commercial or governmental holdings, and that possession of these title deeds makes very little difference to them as they go about their daily business. In London, I own my home and garden; but to do so I have had to call upon the services of lawyers, real-estate dealers, banks and insurance companies, and they will doubtless all be involved again when I move. Boring, uncontroversial – and expensive. But manageable.

But suppose they found gold beneath my back garden. Or oil. Or started mining uranium up the road, which might render them wealthy but my land contaminated. Or suppose somebody got in touch with me and claimed that his or her ancestors had been forcibly evicted from the land I thought mine by a corrupt regime decades (or centuries) ago? This is happening in newly de-communised Eastern Europe all the time. And it is happening in various parts of the world where aboriginal peoples are demanding back the land that they consider unjustly taken from them by white conquerors.

Nowhere are these issues more hotly debated than in Arctic Canada where land claims and aboriginal rights are central to the national agenda. What happens in Canada is closely monitored by native peoples in the United States, Latin America, Australia and elsewhere – and regarded by many white observers with a combination of dismay and incomprehension. Why, they ask, should a native Inuit population of perhaps

30,000 people claim title to so large a land area? It is true that, historically, there was much white abuse of the native Eskimo population of the Canadian (and American) north; but aren't the descendants of those Eskimos being greedy, or even vengeful, in pressing their claim to ownership of so sizeable a proportion of the entire land mass of Canada? Rumours abound of the abundant mineral wealth in the Canadian Arctic, and have done so among Europeans since at least the time of Martin Frobisher's discovery of 'gold' in the 1570s. The Klondike gold rush of the 1890s brought northern mineral mania to fever pitch, and today lead, zinc, gold and uranium are among the metals extracted from Canada's northern territories. There has been oil exploration off Canada's Beaufort Sea coast. Also, despite a currently somewhat depressed market, there are still opportunities for wealth with the sale of skins and furs.

But a desire for wealth *per se* is not what fundamentally underpins native land claims in the Canadian north. Rather, it is an attachment to the land itself. "We have always lived on the land," one local elder told me in a little community far above Canada's Arctic Circle. But nobody is stopping you doing that, I interjected, pointing to the caribou meat drying outside his front door, to his wife's sealskin boots, and to the fact that, as we spoke, his sons were out at camp in the barrenlands hunting and were not expected back for several days. Why did it matter that title to these apparently limitless lands technically rested with the federal government far away down south in Ottawa? If you are free to roam the lands and live off its produce as you have done since time immemorial, why does it matter who owns the land?

He looked at me, patiently, shaking his head. "You see," he began, "we don't want to own the land any more than the birds and the animals, the sun or the moon own it. But it's ours as much as it is theirs. We have inherited temporary use of the land from those who went before us, with a sacred trust from our ancestors to look after it and to preserve it intact for our children and our descendants. We're not owners. We're trustees. Our people have always lived in spiritual harmony with the land. By what right did the *kabloona* come and say this land was his?"

Strong stuff, gently delivered, raising as many questions as it answers. In the early days, the government of Canada was not involved as such. Upper and Lower Canada had their own problems to solve, and federation and self-governing status were not achieved until 1867. Not perhaps entirely coincidentally, 1867 was also the year in which the United States, newly assertive having put behind it the traumas of civil war, bought Alaska ('Russian America') from the Tsars. There was now a vast tract of American territory right up there straddling the Arctic Circle and abutting on to the mountains of the Canadian Yukon territory. Both nations were keen to assert sovereignty over their enormous territories – the United States had just emerged from its four-year Civil War over precisely this issue – and the folklore of each in the later-nineteenth and early-twentieth centuries abounds with tall stories of outlaws and desperadoes in remote territories being chased and perhaps brought to book by representatives of the federal authorities far away. The Canadian Mountie, with his boy-scout hat, handsome red uniform and sturdy steed, is as much a figure of myth as the American sheriff. Thus, the desire to assert political sovereignty came into increasing conflict with the traditional Inuit view of themselves as guardians of the great lands and waterways of the Far North. Nor was Canada alone. By the mid-twentieth century, southern governments all around the Arctic rim were trying to congregate nomadic northerners in artificial new settlements, partly to help feed, house and educate them – but partly too in order to assert a permanent presence on their remote northern lands.

No amount of negotiation is likely to reconcile these two philosophies. "We're still travelling people at heart," said Aslak Johansen Eira, a Sami leader I met in a remote spot in the mountains of northern Norway where he and his family were tending their reindeer herds. "All this land you see, and for hundreds of kilometres south, is ours. That is, we and our reindeer travel through it and live off it, every autumn and spring." And in the heart of Arctic Canada, John Avala, fur-clad as he mushed his dog team, took me out over the apparently limitless frozen tundra where he hunts caribou. "This is our land, always was and always will be," he said with a chuckle, "whatever they say down in Ottawa!"

But the natives of the Far North, while maintaining their belief in their own rights to land, have also learned to play the white man's game. When NATO low-flying jets exercised over Goose Bay in Labrador, local Innu groups protested and made world-wide headlines. Inupiat Eskimos fought to maintain their traditional right to hunt the whale in the teeth of much opposition from the International Whaling Commission – and won. Sami solidarity succeeded in modifying plans to build a dam on the Alta River in Norway intended to bring hydroelectric power to the area but which would have flooded beyond redemption the traditional reindeer migration paths and obliterated at least one Sami village. In Russia, as the constituent elements of the old Soviet Union learn to go their separate ways, the Nentsy and Yakut tribespeople have begun to insist upon their own political and cultural rights.

"We native people have tasted power – and it tastes good!" said the ex-mayor of a small community in northern Alaska looking at me with a broad grin. He should know. The Eskimos of Alaska's North Slope, having initially been inclined to resist the oil companies that wished to drill around Prudhoe Bay, turned about, decided to play capitalism at its own game and, as we have seen, became wealthy as a result.

Thirty years ago, as now, people in Canada's north talked of a possible division of the Territories into a Western and an Eastern Arctic. At that time most of the enthusiasm for division was in the west, in and around the MacKenzie delta. These were the Diefenbaker years, the era when an expansive, go-getting Canada saw its north as the economic wave of the future. There was oil in Norman Wells, gold in Yellowknife and zinc and lead in Echo Bay up on the Great Bear Lake. In 1968, the Americans announced the discovery in Prudhoe Bay off the Beaufort coast of north Alaska of an oil find estimated at eleven billion barrels. Who could say what equivalent wealth might not lie off the coast of the MacKenzie delta?

The west was where the wealth was, or was fabled to be. The Canadian Eastern Arctic, by contrast, appeared less available for potential economic development. For one thing, it was, quite simply, more Arctic. Latitude for latitude, any form of drilling or mining would be harder, or at least more expensive, in the east than in the west. Transportation of men and materials, not to mention of the product itself, would also be more costly. The gold of Yellowknife could be shipped across the Great Slave Lake and thence by reasonably decent year-round roads down to the sorting centres in the south. But coal from Rankin Inlet was a much less attractive prospect.

In addition, there were important differences between the

179

populations of the Western and Eastern Arctic. In the Far Northwest the whites tended predominantly to have come from a rugged western background – miners and oilmen from Alberta or traders from Manitoba for instance. Once up north, they got on with their business in the ways they knew best, keeping to themselves and often having minimal contact with local native populations. The natives were, moreover, extremely diverse with no one group predominating. There was a variety of Indian tribes, each with its own language and culture from Cree and Chipewayan in the south, through Slavey, Dogrib and Guitch'en, and a small group of Eskimos, the Inuvialuit people, up near the Beaufort Sea coast and on some of the more westerly islands of the Canadian archipelago such as Banks or Victoria Island. These indigenous peoples would doubtless stand to gain from Western wealth. But their welfare was hardly considered a major factor by southern speculators eager to translate the Diefenbaker dream into reality.

The Eastern Arctic by contrast contained essentially one native group, the Inuit, who were only now leaving a nomadic, land-based existence to live in towns, and who at that time showed few signs of political or economic sophistication. When southerners dismissed the Canadian Arctic as "great snowy wastes" it was essentially the Eastern Arctic to which they referred. The northwest was neither so snowy nor such a wasteland. Who knew how much gold might still lie up there between Yellowknife and the Yukon, or how far beneath Canadian waters the Alaskan gas and oil bonanza might stretch? And if all that wealth was there for the taking, why not cut loose from the icy wastes of the east, and perhaps get going on the road to eventual provincial status for the Western Arctic? Good hard thinking, 1960s-style.

Thirty years on and the issue of land itself is being faced in Canada. In June 1984, after lengthy negotiations that also had to take into account the claims of the Indian Dene and Métis people, representatives of the Inuvialuit community in the Western Arctic, around the MacKenzie delta and the Beaufort Sea region, signed an agreement with the federal government in Ottawa. Under the terms of the Inuvialuit Final Agreement they ceded their earlier claim to aboriginal title to vast stretches of land in the Canadian northwest. Instead, they accepted a package that included legal title to certain selected areas of land near the Beaufort coast and part of the islands immediately to the north, various rights to hunt, fish and trap and so on – and a financial settlement to be managed by a newly established Inuvialuit Regional Corporation.

Any hopes the negotiators on both sides might have had for a bonanza on the scale of Alaska's Prudhoe Bay along the coast have not been realised. The Canadian township of Tuktoyaktuk up on the Beaufort Sea shows all the signs of a community briefly courted and then deserted by the big oil companies. Indeed, some people in the region hinted to me that the long-protracted land claims negotiations and the compromise settlement reached in 1984 might in themselves have given rise to problems that did not exist before. "People like Esso, Shell and Gulf Oil said they'd prefer to keep out until they knew what the ground rules were," one Inuvik city official told me. "If they were going to invest millions of dollars they wanted to know exactly whom they were dealing with."

For all this, the Inuvialuit Final Agreement has worked out reasonably well in practice, the Regional Corporations have invested and spent money to the benefit of the local native communities, and the Inuvialuit people have regained a degree of pride and cultural identity.

But it is in Canada's Eastern Arctic that the most dramatic political developments of recent years have occurred. No longer do mainstream Canadian politicians think of the Far North merely as a remote arc of sovereignty or source of potential mineral wealth. Today, far higher on the national agenda and much featured in the Canadian media are the recurrent constitutional problems associated with the unity or otherwise of the nation as a whole, and a resurgent concern about the rights of Canada's various native populations. These two central preoccupations come together in the Eastern Arctic where there is still talk of dividing the Northwest Territories into two – but where the driving seat is firmly occupied nowadays by the leaders of a highly politicised Inuit community.

First steps have already been taken to transfer rights to 136,000 square miles of land, stretching from the Ontario border on Hudson Bay up towards the North Pole, to the indigenous Inuit people with a view to establishing in the Eastern Arctic a quasi-autonomous region, 'Nunavut'. Many issues are still unresolved. No sovereign government willingly gives up title to territories or to the resources those territories may contain. Nor does Canadian law, which is based on British and French traditions of individual rights and duties, find it comfortable to recognise ethnic groups as having rights of legal ownership. But the move towards Nunavut, the Inuvialuit Final Agreement in the Western Arctic and agreements the Canadian government has signed with various of its Indian groups represent the most advanced efforts anywhere around the entire Arctic rim by southern sovereign governments to tackle head on the growing demands of their native northern peoples.

Will the establishment of Nunavut prove the wave of the future? If so, will the Arctic rim, like much of the recently decommunised Soviet empire, find itself drawn towards the often deceptive blandishments of cultural nationalism? It is impossible to tell. But perhaps Nunavut might hold aloft a standard for an altogether different set of political priorities. My impression from travelling in the region is that the native people and their leaders, while resolute in their political ambitions, are realistic and limited in their aims. The Nunavut region (like the Canadian Northwest Territories as a whole) is a net importer unlikely to stand on its own feet economically for a long time to come. To achieve this it will not only have to develop its currently very rudimentary infrastructure with money provided from the south, but also forge stronger links with newly resurgent communities all around the Arctic rim. Thus, the creation of Nunavut, far from pulling up the drawbridges of cultural separation, could help lead the way towards a greater degree of circumpolar co-operation.

This is certainly what the logic of history suggests. The older preoccupations of the Arctic rim – sovereignty, defence, mineral exploitation – appear to be receding as new issues take their place. Everywhere nowadays the talk is about (for example) the movement and conservation of animals and of fish, environmental pollution and Arctic haze, climate monitoring, aboriginal rights, the latest hi-tech communications systems, or how best to develop Arctic tourism. These are circumpolar issues requiring co-operative solutions best addressed by the Arctic rim peoples themselves.

Right around the circumpolar North a new spirit can be seen: that of reconciliation rather than enmity between the great sovereign powers, of co-operation between native

182

peoples, of civil rather than military politics. All this represents a major turnaround in a very brief period of time.

Problems remain of course and we have encountered many of them in the course of this book: the debilitating effects that drugs and alcohol, not to mention television and video machines, can inflict upon fragile native cultures; the environmental damage that can be caused by careless economic development; the dangers of global warming so evident in a region with so much ice; and the political uncertainties resulting from the break-up of the Soviet Union. But the first step towards the solution of a problem is to recognise it. And many of the peoples of the Arctic are now fully aware that, perhaps for the first time in history, their fate is inextricably bound up with that of the rest of the planet.

Perhaps it is time the rest of us learned the same lesson. Not so long ago (as we noted at the outset) the Arctic and Antarctic were to most people faraway places of which we knew, and probably needed to know, little or nothing. Today all this has changed. The problems that beset the polar regions are deeply intertwined with those that afflict the temperate and equatorial regions in between. Their solutions, too, are closely related to ours.

Futurologists talk of 'resource wars', suggesting that the major conflicts of the twenty-first century will be fought (as some already have been) by ever larger populations squabbling over limited resources such as oil, food or water. If so, the eyes of the world will turn increasingly to the still undeveloped stocks of hydrocarbons around the Arctic and the controversial ban on mining in Antarctica, the nutrient potential of Antarctic krill stocks and the fact that ninety per cent of the world's fresh water is locked up as ice above Greenland and Antarctica. If the earth's atmosphere continues to warm, it is to the variations in polar ice and climate that all will turn for early indications of the possible effects on the rest of the world. Politically, too, the polar regions have vital lessons for the rest of us. The Antarctic Treaty is one of the great models of international co-operation to have emerged from the often doleful record of twentieth-century political experimentation, while in the Far North, too, a new era of circumpolar co-operation appears to be taking over from the sectoral rivalries of the Cold War and before.

Nobody can be complacent as we approach a new century

which could witness a world population of twelve billion or more. Nor of course am I suggesting that the polar regions contain all the answers. But I do believe that it is time the Arctic and Antarctic came in from the cold, as it were. If we truly value life on earth and wish to bequeath a viable environment to the generations to come, we should think not only 'Green' but also 'White'. For what happens at the poles is integral to the fate of the rest of the planet and all it supports. Their destiny is ours. Together we will survive, or succumb.

APPENDIX: THE ANTARCTIC TREATY

Made 1 December 1959; came into force 23 June 1961.
(The Treaty has no limit on its duration. It may be reviewed, at
the request of a Consultative Party.)
Contracting Parties; in chronological order.

§ *United Kingdom*	*31 May 1960*	1
§ *South Africa*	*21 June 1960*	2
§ *Belgium*	*26 July 1960*	3
§ *Japan*	*4 August 1960*	4
§ *United States of America*	*18 August 1960*	5
§ *Norway*	*24 August 1960*	6
§ *France*	*16 September 1960*	7
§ *New Zealand*	*1 November 1960*	8
§ *Russia* *	*2 November 1960*	9
§ Poland	8 June 1961 (29 July 1977)	10
§ *Argentina*	*23 June 1961*	11
§ *Australia*	*23 June 1961*	12
§ *Chile*	*23 June 1961*	13
Czechoslovakia	14 June 1962	14
Denmark	20 May 1965	15
§ Netherlands	30 March 1967 (19 November 1990)	16
Romania	15 September 1971	17
§ Germany, DDR †	19 November 1974 (5 October 1987)	18
§ Brazil	16 May 1975 (12 September 1983)	19
Bulgaria	11 September 1978	20
§ Germany, BRD †	5 February 1979 (3 March 1981)	21
§ Uruguay	11 January 1980 (7 October 1985)	22
Papua New Guinea ‡	16 March 1981	23
§ Italy	18 March 1981 (5 October 1987)	24
§ Peru	10 April 1981 (9 October 1989)	25
§ Spain	31 March 1982 (21 September 1988)	26
§ China, People's Republic	8 June 1983 (7 October 1985)	27
§ India	19 August 1983 (12 September 1983)	28
Hungary	27 January 1984	29
§ Sweden	24 April 1984 (21 September 1988)	30
§ Finland	15 May 1984 (9 October 1989)	31
Cuba	16 August 1984	32
§ Korea (Seoul)	28 November 1986 (9 October 1989)	33
Greece	8 January 1987	34
Korea (Pyongyang)	21 January 1987	35
Austria	25 August 1987	36
§ Ecuador	15 September 1987 (19 November 1990)	37
Canada	4 May 1988	38
Colombia	31 January 1989	39
Switzerland	15 November 1990	40
Guatemala	31 July 1991	41

Original signatories; the 12 states which signed the Treaty on 1 December 1959, are
italicised; the dates given are those of the deposition of the instruments of ratification,
approval, or acceptance of the Treaty.
§ Consultative Parties; 26 states, the 12 original signatories and 14 others (formerly 15)
which achieved this status after becoming actively involved in Antarctic research (with
dates in brackets).
‡ Papua New Guinea succeeded to the Treaty after becoming independent of Australia.
(Some former Soviet Union states may similarly succeed.)
† The two German states unified on 3 October 1990. Thus there are now 40 member states
from the 41 adherents.
* Formerly the Soviet Union, represented by Russia from December 1991.
The above information was supplied by R. K. Headland, Scott Polar Research Institute, in
September 1992.

Index

Illustrations are indicated in bold type

188

189